KNITTED
FOREST FRIENDS

T0405554

KNITTED
FOREST FRIENDS

20 adorable animals to make

SARAH KEEN

THE GUILD OF MASTER CRAFTSMAN PUBLICATIONS

CONTENTS

INTRODUCTION

It has been a pleasurable time designing these knitted forest friends: twenty more adorable animals to accompany those in my previous book, *Knitted Farm Friends*. All the animals are simple and soon knitted, and I hope you find enjoyment in whichever animals you decide to recreate.

DEER 16

BADGER 24

SQUIRREL 30

OWL 36

WILD BOAR 42

BEAVER 50

RACOON 58

HEDGEHOG 64

CUCKOO 70

ANT 76

BEAR 82

KOALA 88

GIANT PANDA 94

WOODPECKER 100

MOUSE 106

FROG 114

WOLF 122

OTTER 134

KIWI 128

ORANGUTAN 140

DEER

INFORMATION YOU'LL NEED

MATERIALS

Any DK (US: light worsted) yarn
(amounts given are approximate)
Yarn A pale brown (20g for each deer)
Yarn B cream (10g)
Yarn C dark brown (10g)
Yarn D pale blue (15g)
Yarn E pale pink (15g)
Yarn F fawn (5g)
Oddments of black and cream for
embroidery and dark brown for making up
1 pair of 3.25mm (UK10:US3) needles and
a spare needle of same size for dungarees
Knitters' pins and a blunt-ended needle
for sewing up
Acrylic toy stuffing
2 small buttons for each deer
1 chenille stem for each deer

FINISHED SIZE

Deer stands 8¼in (21cm) tall

TENSION

26 sts x 34 rows measure 4in (10cm)
square over st-st using 3.25mm needles
and DK yarn before stuffing.

ABBREVIATIONS

See page 156

HOW TO MAKE DEER

BODY
Using the long tail method and yarn A, cast on 32 sts.
Row 1: Purl.
Row 2: K1, (k7, m1, k1, m1, k7) twice, k1 (36 sts).
Rows 3 to 9: Work 7 rows in st-st.
Rows 10 and 11: Work 2 rows in g-st to mark waist.
Rows 12 to 21: Beg with a k row, work 10 rows in st-st.
Row 22: K1, (k7, k3tog, k7) twice, k1 (32 sts).
Row 23 and foll alt row: Purl.
Row 24: K1, (k6, k3tog, k6) twice, k1 (28 sts).
Row 26: K1, (k5, k3tog, k5) twice, k1 (24 sts).
Row 27: Purl.
Cast off.

HEAD
Using the long tail method and yarn B, cast on 8 sts.
Row 1 and foll alt row: Purl.
Row 2: (Kfb) to end (16 sts).
Row 4: (Kfb) to end (32 sts).
Join on yarn A and work in yarn A and yarn B, carrying yarn B loosely behind yarn A and twisting yarn when changing colours to avoid a hole.
Row 5: Yarn B-p14, yarn A-p4, yarn B-p14.
Row 6: Yarn B-k14, yarn A-k4, yarn B-k14.
Row 7: As row 5.

Row 8: Yarn B-(k3, kfb) 3 times, k2, yarn A-k4, yarn B-k2, (kfb, k3) 3 times (38 sts).
Row 9: Yarn B-p17, yarn A-p4, yarn B-p17.
Row 10: Yarn B-k17, yarn A-k1, m1, k2, m1, k1, yarn B-k17 (40 sts).
Row 11: Yarn B-p17, yarn A-p6, yarn B-p17.
Rows 12 to 21: Rejoin yarn A and cont in yarn A and work 10 rows in st-st.
Row 22: (K2tog, k3) to end (32 sts).
Row 23 and foll 2 alt rows: Purl.
Row 24: (K2tog, k2) to end (24 sts).
Row 26: (K2tog, k1) to end (16 sts).
Row 28: (K2tog) to end (8 sts).
Break yarn and thread through sts on needle, pull tight and secure by threading yarn a second time through sts.

SNOUT
Using the long tail method and yarn A, cast on 21 sts.
Rows 1 to 5: Beg with a p row, work 5 rows in st-st.
Row 6: (K2tog, k1) to end (14 sts).
Row 7: Purl.
Row 8: (K2tog) to end (7 sts).
Break yarn and thread through sts on needle, pull tight and secure by threading yarn a second time through sts.

TROTTERS AND LEGS
(make 2)
Using the long tail method and yarn C, cast on 8 sts.

Row 1 and foll alt row: Purl.

Row 2: (Kfb) to end (16 sts).

Row 4: (Kfb, k1) to end (24 sts).

Rows 5 to 9: Work 5 rows in st-st.

Change to yarn B and dec:

Row 10: (K2tog, k1) to end (16 sts).

Rows 11 to 13: Work 3 rows in st-st.

Rows 14 to 25: Change to yarn A and work 12 rows in st-st.

Cast off.

TROTTERS AND FOREARMS (make 2)
Using the long tail method and yarn C, cast on 8 sts.

Row 1: Purl.

Row 2: (Kfb) to end (16 sts).

Rows 3 to 7: Work 5 rows in st-st.

Change to yarn B and dec:

Row 8: K2, k2tog, (k3, k2tog) twice, k2 (13 sts).

Rows 9 to 11: Work 3 rows in st-st.

Rows 12 to 25: Change to yarn A and work 14 rows in st-st.

Row 26: K1, (k2tog, k1) to end (9 sts).

Break yarn, thread through sts on needle and leave loose.

DUNGAREES
(make 2 pieces)
Note: foll individual instructions as given for 1 front and 1 back of dungarees.

FIRST LEG
Using the long tail method and yarn D, cast on 12 sts and beg in g-st.

Rows 1 and 2: Work 2 rows in g-st.

Break yarn and set aside.

SECOND LEG
Work as for first leg but do not break yarn.

JOIN LEGS
Row 3: Beg with second leg and k10, k2tog, turn, using the knitting-on method cast on 5 sts, turn, then with the same yarn continue across first leg and k2tog, k to end (27 sts).

Rows 4 to 6: Beg with a p row, work 3 rows in st-st.

Row 7: K11, k2tog, k1, k2tog, k11 (25 sts).

Row 8: Purl.

Row 9: K9, k2tog, k3, k2tog, k9 (23 sts).

Rows 10 to 14: Work 5 rows in st-st.

Rows 15 to 17: Work 3 rows in g-st, ending with a RS row.

Cast off in g-st for back of dungarees or cont with bib for front of dungarees:

DIVIDE FOR BIB
Row 18: Cast off 6 sts kwise, k10 (11 sts now on RH needle), cast

off rem 6 sts and fasten off.
Rejoin yarn to rem sts and patt:
Row 19: K2, (k1 tbl) 7 times, k2
(11 sts).
Row 20: K2, p7, k2.
Row 21: Knit.
Rows 22 to 27: Rep rows 20 and
21, 3 times more, ending with a
k row.
Rows 28 and 29: Work 2 rows in
g-st, ending with a RS row.
Cast off in g-st.

STRAPS FOR DUNGAREES (make 2)

Using the long tail method and
yarn D, cast on 26 sts.
Row 1: Knit.
Cast off kwise.

PINAFORE

Using the long tail method and
yarn E, cast on 60 sts and beg
in g-st.
Rows 1 and 2: Work 2 rows
in g-st.
Rows 3 to 12: Beg with a k row,
work 10 rows in st-st.
Row 13: K1, (k2tog, k2) to last
3 sts, k2tog, k1 (45 sts).
Rows 14 and 15: Work 2 rows in
g-st, ending with a RS row.
DIVIDE FOR BIB
Row 16: Cast off 17 sts kwise,
k10 (11 sts now on RH needle),
cast off rem 17 sts and fasten off.
Rejoin yarn to rem sts and work
bib from **, as for dungarees.

STRAPS FOR PINAFORE

Make straps using yarn E, as for
dungarees.

ANTLERS (make 2)
MAIN PIECE
Using the long tail method and
yarn F, cast on 8 sts.
Rows 1 to 11: Beg with a p row,
work 11 rows in st-st.
Break yarn and thread through
sts on needle, pull tight and
secure by threading yarn a
second time through sts.
SIDE PIECE
Using the long tail method and F,
cast on 8 sts.
Rows 1 to 3: Beg with a p row,
work 3 rows in st-st.
Break yarn and thread through
sts on needle, pull tight and
secure by threading yarn a
second time through sts.

EARS (make 2)
Using the long tail method and
yarn A, cast on 10 sts.
Row 1: Purl.
Row 2: K2, (m1, k2) to end
(14 sts).
Rows 3 to 7: Work 5 rows in st-st.
Row 8: (K2tog) to end (7 sts).
Rows 9 to 11: Work 3 rows
in st-st.
Break yarn and thread through
sts on needle, pull tight and
secure by threading yarn a
second time through sts.

MAKING UP

Note: Sew up all row-end seams on right side using mattress stitch one stitch in from the edge, unless otherwise stated; a one-stitch seam allowance has been allowed for this.

BODY

Sew up side edges of body and with this seam at centre back, oversew cast-on stitches. Stuff body leaving neck open.

HEAD AND SNOUT

Weave in ends around colour work. Gather round cast-on stitches of head, pull tight and secure. Sew up side edges of head leaving a gap, stuff head and sew up gap. Pin head to body, matching pale brown at back of neck, and sew head to body. Sew up side edges of snout and stuff. Pin and sew snout to front of head.

TROTTERS AND LEGS

Gather round cast-on stitches of trotters, pull tight and secure. Sew up side edges of trotters and legs, stuff trotters then stuff legs. Pin legs to body leaving a ¾in (2cm) gap at crotch and sew in place. Shape trotters using dark brown and embroider a loop around centre of trotters, pull tight, then go a second time around and secure.

TROTTERS AND FOREARMS

Gather round cast-on stitches of trotters, pull tight and secure. Sew up side edges of trotters and forearms, stuff trotters then stuff forearms. Pull stitches on a thread tight and secure. Sew forearms to Deer at each side. Shape trotters in dark brown, as for legs.

DUNGAREES, STRAPS AND BUTTONS

Place two pieces of dungarees together matching all edges, sew up inside leg seams and across crotch. Sew up side seams and place dungarees on Deer. Sew cast-off stitches of waist of dungarees to row above waist of Deer using backstitch. Sew ends of straps to top edge of front of bib, take straps over shoulders, cross over and sew to back of dungarees. Add two buttons to bib.

PINAFORE, STRAPS AND BUTTONS

Sew up side edges of skirt of pinafore and place pinafore on Deer. Sew cast-off stitches of waist of pinafore to row above waist of Deer using backstitch. Sew ends of straps to top edge of front of bib, take straps over shoulders, cross over and sew to back of pinafore. Add two buttons to bib.

ANTLERS

Fold a chenille stem in half and place fold into stitches pulled tight on a thread of main piece of antler. Sew up side edges of antler enclosing chenille stem inside. Sew up side edges of side piece and sew side piece to inside of antler at right angles. Cut excess chenille stem, repeat for other antler and sew antlers to head.

EARS

Oversew side edges of ears and with this seam at centre back, fold cast-on stitches of ears in half and sew in place. Position ears and pin and sew ears to Deer.

FEATURES

Mark position of eyes with two pins and embroider eyes in black making a vertical chain stitch for each eye, then a second chain stitch on top of first, then embroider a horizontal line on outside edge of each eye using straight stitches. Embroider nose in black using satin stitch and embroider eyebrows and mouth using straight stitches. Embroider spots on top of head in cream using 'V'-shape straight stitches (see page 155 for how to begin and fasten off invisibly for the embroidery).

BADGER

INFORMATION YOU'LL NEED

MATERIALS
Any DK (US: light worsted) yarn
(amounts given are approximate)
Yarn A dark grey (10g)
Yarn B white (10g)
Yarn C black (15g)
Yarn D soft red (10g)
Oddment of grey for embroidery
1 pair of 3.25mm (UK10:US3)
needles and a spare needle of
same size
3 knitters' bobbins
Knitters' pins and a blunt-ended
needle for sewing up
Acrylic toy stuffing
2 small buttons

FINISHED SIZE
Badger stands 7in (18cm) tall

TENSION
26 sts x 34 rows measure 4in (10cm)
square over st-st using 3.25mm
needles and DK yarn before stuffing.

ABBREVIATIONS
See page 156

HOW TO MAKE BADGER

BODY

Using the long tail method and yarn A, cast on 36 sts.

Row 1: Purl.

Row 2: K1, (k8, m1, k1, m1, k8) twice, k1 (40 sts).

Rows 3 to 9: Work 7 rows in st-st.

Rows 10 and 11: Work 2 rows in g-st to mark waist.

Rows 12 to 19: Beg with a k row, work 8 rows in st-st.

Row 20: K1, (k8, k3tog, k8) twice, k1 (36 sts).

Row 21 and foll 2 alt rows: Purl.

Row 22: K1, (k7, k3tog, k7) twice, k1 (32 sts).

Row 24: K1, (k6, k3tog, k6) twice, k1 (28 sts).

Row 26: K1, (k5, k3tog, k5) twice, k1 (24 sts).

Row 27: Purl.

Cast off.

HEAD

Note: Before beg, wind 2 bobbins in yarn B and 2 bobbins in yarn C and reserve.

Using the long tail method and yarn B, cast on 8 sts.

Row 1 and foll 3 alt rows: Purl.

Row 2: (Kfb) to end (16 sts).

Row 4: (Kfb, k1) to end (24 sts).

Row 6: (Kfb, k2) to end (32 sts).

Row 8: (Kfb, k3) to end (40 sts).

Rows 9 to 11: Work 3 rows in st-st.

Join on 2 bobbins of yarns B and C and work in intarsia in blocks of colours, twisting yarn when changing colours to avoid a hole:

Row 12: Yarn B-k12, yarn C (first bobbin)-k5, yarn B (first bobbin)-k6, yarn C (second bobbin)-k5, yarn B (second bobbin)-k12.

Row 13: Yarn B-p12, yarn C-p5, yarn B-p6, yarn C-p5, yarn B-p12.

Rows 14 to 17: Rep rows 12 and 13 twice more.

Row 18: Yarn B- k12, yarn C-k5, yarn B-k2, k2tog, k2, yarn C-k5, yarn B-k12 (39 sts).

Row 19: Yarn B-p12, yarn C-p5, yarn B-p5, yarn C-p5, yarn B-p12.

Row 20: Yarn B-(K2tog, k2) 3 times, yarn C-k1, k2tog, k2, yarn B-k5, C-k2, k2tog, k1, B-(k2, k2tog) 3 times (31 sts).

Row 21: Yarn B-p9, yarn C-p4, yarn B-p5, yarn C-p4, yarn B-p9.

Row 22: Yarn B-k1, (k2tog, k2) twice, yarn C-k4, yarn B-k5, yarn C-k4, yarn B-(k2, k2tog), twice, k1 (27 sts).

Row 23: Yarn B-p7, yarn C-p4, yarn B-p5, yarn C-p4, yarn B-p7.

Row 24: Yarn B-k1, (k2tog, k1) twice, yarn C-k1, k2tog, k1, yarn B-k2tog, k1, k2tog, yarn C-k1, k2tog, k1, yarn B-(K1, k2tog) twice, k1 (19 sts).

Row 25: Yarn B-p5, yarn C-p3, yarn B-p3, yarn C-p3, yarn B-p5.

Row 26: Yarn B-k5, yarn C-k3, yarn B-k3, yarn C-k3, yarn B-k5.

Row 27: As row 25.

Work next 2 rows in yarn B and shape:

Row 28: K2tog, (k1, k2tog) twice, k3, (k2tog, k1) twice, k2tog (13 sts).

Row 29: Purl.

Change to yarn C and shape:

Row 30: K1, (k2tog, k1) to end (9 sts).

Rows 31 and 32: Cont in rev st-st and k 1 row then p 1 row.

Break yarn and thread through sts on needle, pull tight and secure by threading yarn a second time through sts.

FEET AND LEGS (make 2)

Using the long tail method and yarn C, cast on 16 sts.

Row 1: Purl.

Row 2: (K1, kfb) 4 times, (kfb, k1) 4 times (24 sts).

Rows 3 to 9: Work 7 rows in st-st.

Row 10: K6, (k2tog) 6 times, k6 (18 sts).

Row 11: Purl.

Row 12: K7, (k2tog) twice, k7 (16 sts).

Rows 13 to 17: Work 5 rows in st-st.

Cast off.

PAWS AND FOREARMS
(make 2)

Using the long tail method and yarn C, cast on 10 sts.

Row 1: Purl.

Row 2: (Kfb) to end (20 sts).

Rows 3 to 7: Work 5 rows in st-st.

Row 8: (K2tog, k2) to end (15 sts).

Rows 9 to 19: Work 11 rows in st-st.

Row 20: (K2tog, k1) to end (10 sts).

Break yarn, thread through sts on needle and leave loose.

DUNGAREES
(make 2 pieces)

Note: foll individual instructions as given for 1 front and 1 back of dungarees.

FIRST LEG

Using the long tail method and yarn D, cast on 12 sts and beg in g-st.

Rows 1 and 2: Work 2 rows in g-st.

Break yarn and set aside.

SECOND LEG

Work as for first leg but do not break yarn.

JOIN LEGS

Row 3: Beg with second leg and k10, k2tog, turn, using the knitting-on method cast on 5 sts, turn, then with the same yarn continue across first leg and k2tog, k to end (27 sts).

Row 4 and foll 2 alt rows: Purl.

Row 5: K2, m1, k23, m1, k2 (29 sts).

Row 7: K12, k2tog, k1, k2tog, k12 (27 sts).

Row 9: K10, k2tog, k3, k2tog, k10 (25 sts).

Rows 10 to 14: Work 5 rows in st-st.

Rows 15 to 17: Work 3 rows in g-st, ending with a RS row.

Cast off in g-st for back of dungarees or cont with bib for front of dungarees:

DIVIDE FOR BIB

Row 18: Cast off 6 sts kwise, k12 (13 sts now on RH needle), cast off rem 6 sts and fasten off. Rejoin yarn to rem sts and patt:

Row 19: K2, (k1 tbl) 9 times, k2 (13 sts).

Row 20: K2, p9, k2.

Row 21: Knit.

Rows 22 to 27: Rep rows 20 and 21, 3 times more, ending with a k row.

Rows 28 and 29: Work 2 rows in g-st, ending with a RS row.

Cast off in g-st.

STRAPS FOR DUNGAREES
(make 2)

Using the long tail method and yarn D, cast on 26 sts.

Row 1: Knit.

Cast off kwise.

EARS (make 2)

Note: Before beg, wind 1 bobbin in yarn C and reserve.

Using the long tail method and yarn C, cast on 16 sts.

Join on yarn B and bobbin of yarn C and work in intarsia in blocks of colour, twisting yarn when changing colours to avoid a hole:

Row 1: Yarn C-p6, yarn B-p4, yarn C (bobbin)-p6.

Row 2: Yarn C-k6, yarn B-k4, yarn C-k6.

Row 3: As row 1.

Row 4: Yarn C-k2, k2tog, k2, yarn B-k1, k2tog, k1, yarn C-k2, k2tog, k2 (13 sts).

Row 5: Cont in yarn C and p 1 row.

Row 6: K2tog, k1, k2tog, k3, k2tog, k1, k2tog (9 sts).

Break yarn and thread through sts on needle, pull tight and secure by threading yarn a second time through sts.

MAKING UP

Note: Sew up all row-end seams on right side using mattress stitch one stitch in from the edge, unless otherwise stated; a one-stitch seam allowance has been allowed for this.

BODY

Sew up side edges of body and with this seam at centre back, oversew cast-on stitches. Stuff body leaving neck open.

HEAD

Weave in ends around intarsia. Gather round cast-on stitches, pull tight and secure. Sew up side edges of head leaving a gap, stuff, pushing stuffing into nose and sew up gap. Pin and sew head to body making a short stitch over one stitch from head, then a short stitch over one stitch from body, and do this alternately all the way round.

FEET AND LEGS

Fold cast-on stitches of feet in half and oversew. Sew up side edges of legs and stuff feet and legs. Pin legs to body leaving a ¾in (2cm) gap at crotch and sew in place.

PAWS AND FOREARMS

Gather round cast-on stitches of forearms, pull tight and secure. Sew up side edges of paws and stuff paws. Sew up side edges of forearms, stuff, and pull stitches on a thread tight and secure. Sew forearms to Badger at each side.

DUNGAREES, STRAPS AND BUTTONS

Make up dungarees, straps and buttons, as for Deer on page 22.

EARS

Sew up side edges of ears and with this seam at centre back, press flat. Position ears and pin and sew ears to head.

FEATURES

Mark position of eyes with two pins and embroider eyes in grey, making a vertical chain stitch for each eye, then a second chain stitch on top of first. Embroider eyebrows in grey using straight stitches (see page 155 for how to begin and fasten off invisibly for the embroidery).

SQUIRREL

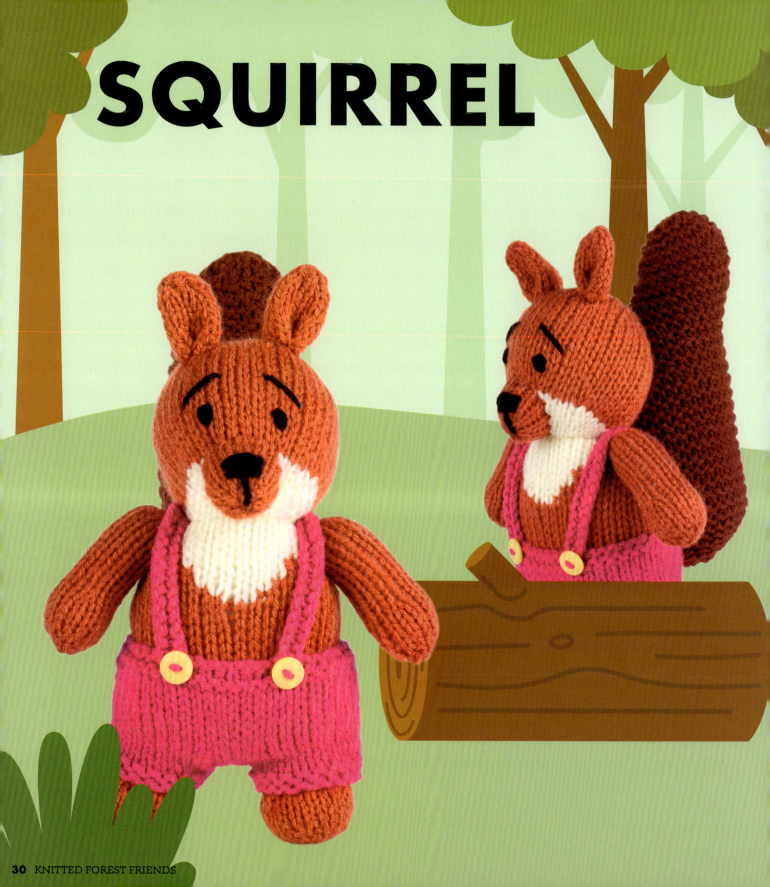

INFORMATION YOU'LL NEED

MATERIALS
Any DK (US: light worsted) yarn
(amounts given are approximate)
Yarn A pale ginger (20g)
Yarn B cream (5g)
Yarn C cerise (10g)
Yarn D ginger brown (15g)
Oddment of black for embroidery
1 pair of 3.25mm (UK10:US3)
needles and a spare needle of
same size
1 yarn bobbin
Knitters' pins and a blunt-ended
needle for sewing up
Acrylic toy stuffing
2 small buttons

FINISHED SIZE
Squirrel stands 8in (20.5cm) tall

TENSION
26 sts x 34 rows measure 4in (10cm)
square over st-st using 3.25mm
needles and DK yarn before stuffing.

ABBREVIATIONS
See page 156

HOW TO MAKE SQUIRREL

BODY

Note: before beg, wind a bobbin in yarn A and reserve.

Using the long tail method and yarn A, cast on 36 sts.

Row 1: Purl.

Row 2: K1, (k8, m1, k1, m1, k8) twice, k1 (40 sts).

Rows 3 to 11: Work 9 rows in st-st.

Rows 12 and 13: Work 2 rows in g-st to mark waist.

Rows 14 to 19: Beg with a k row, work 6 rows in st-st.

Join on yarn B and bobbin of yarn A and work in intarsia in blocks of colour, twisting yarn when changing colours to avoid a hole.

Row 20: Yarn A-k19, yarn B-k2, yarn A (bobbin)-k19.

Row 21: Yarn A-p18, yarn B-p4, yarn A-p18.

Row 22: Yarn A-k9, k3tog, k5, yarn B-k6, yarn A-k5, k3tog, k9 (36 sts).

Row 23: Yarn A-p15, yarn B-p6, yarn A-p15.

Row 24: Yarn A-k8, k3tog, k3, yarn B-k8, yarn A-k3, k3tog, k8 (32 sts).

Row 25: Yarn A-p12, yarn B-p8, yarn A-p12.

Row 26: Yarn A-k7, k3tog, k1, yarn B-k10, yarn A-k1, k3tog, k7 (28 sts).

Row 27: Yarn A-p9, yarn B-p10, yarn A-p9.

Row 28: Yarn A-k6, k3tog, yarn B-k10, yarn A-k3tog, k6 (24 sts).

Row 29: Yarn A-p7, yarn B-p10, yarn A-p7.

Cast off in colours as set.

HEAD

Using the long tail method and yarn A, cast on 8 sts.

Row 1 and foll 3 alt rows: Purl.

Row 2: (Kfb) to end (16 sts).

Row 4: (Kfb, k1) to end (24 sts).

Row 6: (Kfb, k2) to end (32 sts).

Row 8: (Kfb, k3) to end (40 sts).

Rows 9 to 21: Work 13 rows in st-st.

Change to yarn B and dec:

Row 22: (K2tog, k3) to end (32 sts).

Row 23 and foll 2 alt rows: Purl.

Row 24: (K2tog, k2) to end (24 sts).

Row 26: (K2tog, k1) to end (16 sts).

Row 28: (K2tog) to end (8 sts).

Break yarn and thread through sts on needle, pull tight and secure by threading yarn a second time through sts.

SNOUT

Using the long tail method and yarn A, cast on 16 sts.

Rows 1 to 5: Beg with a p row, work 5 rows in st-st.

Row 6: (K2tog) to end (8 sts).

Break yarn and thread through sts on needle, pull tight and secure by threading yarn a second time through sts.

FEET AND LEGS (make 2)

Using the long tail method and yarn A, cast on 16 sts.

Row 1: Purl.

Row 2: (K1, kfb) 4 times, (kfb, k1) 4 times (24 sts).

Rows 3 to 7: Work 5 rows in st-st.

Row 8: K4, (k2tog) 8 times, k4 (16 sts).

Rows 9 to 13: Work 5 rows in st-st.

Cast off.

PAWS AND FOREARMS (make 2)

Using the long tail method and yarn A, cast on 8 sts.

Row 1: Purl.

Row 2: (Kfb) to end (16 sts).

Rows 3 to 7: Work 5 rows in st-st.

Row 8: (K2tog, k2) to end (12 sts).

Rows 9 to 21: Work 13 rows in st-st.

Row 22: (K2tog, k1) to end (8 sts).

Break yarn, thread through sts on needle and leave loose.

TROUSERS (make 2 pieces)

FIRST LEG

Using the long tail method and yarn C, cast on 12 sts and beg in g-st.

Rows 1 and 2: Work 2 rows in g-st.

Break yarn and set aside.

SECOND LEG

Work as for first leg but do not break yarn.

JOIN LEGS

Row 3: Beg with second leg and k10, k2tog, turn, using the knitting-on method cast on 5 sts, turn, then with the same yarn continue across first leg and k2tog, k to end (27 sts).

Row 4 and foll 2 alt rows: Purl.

Row 5: K2, m1, k23, m1, k2 (29 sts).

Row 7: K12, k2tog, k1, k2tog, k12 (27 sts).

Row 9: K10, k2tog, k3, k2tog, k10 (25 sts).

Rows 10 to 16: Work 7 rows in st-st.

Rows 17 to 19: Work 3 rows in g-st, ending with a RS row. Cast off in g-st.

BRACES (make 2)

Using the long tail method and yarn C, cast on 32 sts.

Row 1: Knit.
Cast off kwise.

EARS (make 2)

Using the long tail method and yarn A, cast on 10 sts.

Row 1: Purl.

Row 2: K1, (m1, k1) to end (19 sts).

Rows 3 to 5: Work 3 rows in st-st.

Row 6: K1, (k2tog, k1) to end (13 sts).

Rows 7 to 9: Work 3 rows in st-st.

Row 10: K1, (k2tog, k1) to end (9 sts).

Row 11: Purl.
Break yarn and thread through sts on needle, pull tight and secure by threading yarn a second time through sts.

TAIL

Using the long tail method and yarn D, cast on 8 sts and work in g-st.

Rows 1 and 2: Work 2 rows in g-st.

Row 3: (Kfb) to end (16 sts).

Rows 4 to 6: Work 3 rows in g-st.

Row 7: (Kfb, k1) to end (24 sts).

Rows 8 to 10: Work 3 rows in g-st.

Row 11: (Kfb, k2) to end (32 sts).

Rows 12 to 42: Work 31 rows in g-st.

Row 43: (K2tog) twice, k10, (kfb) 4 times, k10, (k2tog) twice.

Rows 44 to 46: Work 3 rows in g-st.

Rows 47 to 58: Rep rows 43 to 46, 3 times more.

Row 59: (K2tog, k2) to end (24 sts).

Row 60: Knit.

Row 61: (K2tog, k1) to end (16 sts).

Rows 62 and 63: Work 2 rows in g-st.

Row 64: (K2tog) to end (8 sts).
Break yarn and thread through sts on needle, pull tight and secure by threading yarn a second time through sts.

MAKING UP

Note: Sew up all row-end seams on right side using mattress stitch one stitch in from the edge, unless otherwise stated; a one-stitch seam allowance has been allowed for this.

BODY

Weave in ends around intarsia. Sew up side edges of body and with this seam at centre back, oversew cast-on stitches. Stuff body leaving neck open.

HEAD AND SNOUT

Gather round cast-on stitches of head, pull tight and secure. Sew up side edges of head leaving a gap, stuff head and sew up gap. Pin and sew head to body matching up cream with neck of body. Sew up side edges of snout, stuff, and pin and sew snout to head.

FEET AND LEGS

Fold cast on stitches of feet in half and oversew. Sew up side edges of feet and legs and stuff. Pin legs to body with toes pointing outwards, leaving a ¾in (2cm) gap at crotch, and sew in place.

PAWS AND FOREARMS

Gather round cast-on stitches of paws, pull tight and secure. Sew up side edges of paws and place a small ball of stuffing into paws. Sew up side edges of arms, stuff, and pull stitches on a thread tight and secure. Sew forearms to squirrel at each side.

TROUSERS, BRACES AND BUTTONS

Place two pieces of trousers together matching all edges, sew up inside leg seams and across crotch. Sew up side seams and place trousers on Squirrel. Sew cast-off stitches of trousers to row above waist using backstitch. Sew ends of braces to front of trousers, take braces over shoulders, cross over and sew ends to back waist, and sew braces in place. Add two buttons to front of trousers.

EARS

Sew up side edges of ears and with seam at centre front, press flat. Fold cast-on stitches of ears in half and sew in place. Position ears and pin and sew ears to head.

FEATURES

Mark position of eyes with two pins and embroider eyes in black making a vertical chain stitch for each eye, then a second chain stitch on top of first. Embroider eyebrows in black using long stitches. Embroider nose in black using satin stitch and a vertical straight stitch (see page 155 for how to begin and fasten off invisibly for the embroidery).

TAIL

Gather round cast-on stitches of tail, pull tight and secure. Oversew row ends of tail, leaving a gap, stuff and sew up gap. Sew tail to back of Squirrel.

OWL

INFORMATION YOU'LL NEED

MATERIALS
Any DK (US: light worsted) yarn
(amounts given are approximate)
Yarn A pale brown (20g)
Yarn B cream (10g)
Yarn C dark brown (5g)
Yarn D mustard (5g)
Yarn E orange (10g)
Yarn F black (5g)
1 pair of 3.25mm (UK10:US3)
needles and a spare needle of
same size
Knitters' pins and a blunt-ended
needle for sewing up
Tweezers (optional)
Acrylic toy stuffing
2 small buttons

FINISHED SIZE
Owl stands 7in (18cm) tall

TENSION
26 sts x 34 rows measure 4in
(10cm) square over st-st using
3.25mm needles and DK yarn
before stuffing.

ABBREVIATIONS
See page 156

HOW TO MAKE OWL

BODY AND HEAD

Using the long tail method and yarn A, cast on 44 sts.

Row 1: Purl.

Row 2: K1, (k10, m1, k1, m1, k10) twice, k1 (48 sts).

Rows 3 to 9: Work 7 rows in st-st.

Rows 10 and 11: Work 2 rows in g-st to mark waist.

Rows 12 to 27: Beg with a k row, work 16 rows in st-st.

Row 28: K1, (k10, k3tog, k10) twice, k1 (44 sts).

Row 29 and foll alt row: Purl.

Row 30: K1, (k9, k3tog, k9) twice, k1 (40 sts).

Row 32: K1, (k8, k3tog, k8) twice, k1 (36 sts).

Rows 33 to 45: Work 13 rows in st-st.

Row 46: K1, (k7, m1, k3, m1, k7) twice, k1 (40 sts).

Row 47 and foll alt row: Purl.

Row 48: K1, (k8, m1, k3, m1, k8) twice, k1 (44 sts).

Row 50: K1, (k9, m1, k3, m1, k9) twice, k1 (48 sts).

Rows 51 to 53: Work 3 rows in st-st.

Cast off.

TUMMY

Using the long tail method and yarn B, cast on 26 sts and work in g-st.

Join on yarn C and work in stripes, carrying yarn loosely up side of work.

Rows 1 and 2: Using yarn C, work 2 rows in g-st.

Rows 3 and 4: Using yarn B, work 2 rows in g-st.

Rows 5 to 12: Rep rows 1 to 4 twice more.

Row 13: Using yarn C, k2tog, k to last 2 sts, k2tog (24 sts).

Row 14: As row 13 (22 sts).

Row 15: Using yarn B, k2tog, k to last 2 sts, k2tog (20 sts).

Row 16: As row 15 (18 sts).

Rows 17 to 20: Rep rows 13 to 16 once (10 sts).

Row 21: Using yarn C, k2tog, k to last 2 sts, k2tog (8 sts).

Cast off in yarn C.

LEGS (make 2)

Using the long tail method and yarn D, cast on 8 sts.

Row 1: Purl.

Row 2: (Kfb) to end (16 sts).

Rows 3 to 9: Work 7 rows in st-st.

Cast off.

TROUSERS (make 2 pieces)

FIRST LEG

Using the long tail method and yarn E, cast on 10 sts and beg in g-st.

Rows 1 and 2: Work 2 rows in g-st.

Break yarn and set aside.

SECOND LEG

Work as for first leg but do not break yarn.

JOIN LEGS

Row 3: Beg with second leg and k8, k2tog, turn, using the knitting-on method cast on 5 sts, turn, then with the same yarn continue across first leg and k2tog, k to end (23 sts).

Row 4 and foll 2 alt rows: Purl.

Row 5: (K2, m1) twice, k15, (m1, k2) twice (27 sts).

Row 7: (K2, m1) twice, k7, k2tog, k1, k2tog, k7, (m1, k2) twice (29 sts).

Row 9: K11, k2tog, k3, k2tog, k11 (27 sts).

Rows 10 to 14: Work 5 rows in st-st.

Rows 15 to 17: Work 3 rows in g-st ending with a RS row.

Cast off in g-st.

FEET AND BACK TOE (make 2)

Using the long tail method and yarn D, cast on 15 sts.

Rows 1 to 3: Beg with a p row, work 3 rows in st-st.

Row 4: K3, k2tog, k5, k2tog, k3 (13 sts).

Rows 5 to 7: Work 3 rows in st-st.

Row 8: K3, k2tog, k3, k2tog, k3 (11 sts).

Rows 9 to 11: Work 3 rows in st-st.

Row 12: K2, k2tog, k3, k2tog, k2 (9 sts).

Rows 13 to 15: Work 3 rows in st-st.

Break yarn and thread through sts on needle, pull tight and secure by threading yarn a second time through sts.

TOES (make 6)

Using the long tail method and yarn D, cast on 8 sts.

Rows 1 to 3: Beg with a p row, work 3 rows in st-st.

Break yarn and thread through sts on needle, pull tight and secure by threading yarn a second time through sts.

WINGS (make 2)

Using the long tail method and yarn A, cast on 22 sts.

Row 1: Purl.

Row 2: K2, (m1, k2) to end (32 sts).

Rows 3 to 13: Work 11 rows in st-st.

Row 14: K4, (k2tog) twice, k16, (k2tog) twice, k4 (28 sts).

Row 15 and foll 5 alt rows: Purl.

Row 16: K4, (k2tog) twice, k12, (k2tog) twice, k4 (24 sts).

Row 18: K2, (k2tog) twice, k12, (k2tog) twice, k2 (20 sts).

Row 20: K2, (k2tog) twice, k8, (k2tog) twice, k2 (16 sts).

Row 22: (K2tog) twice, k8, (k2tog) twice (12 sts).

Row 24: (K2tog) twice, k4, (k2tog) twice (8 sts).

Row 26: (K2tog) to end (4 sts).

Break yarn and thread through sts on needle, pull tight and secure by threading yarn a second time through sts.

EYE PATCHES (make 2)

Using the long tail method and yarn B, cast on 30 sts.

Rows 1 and 2: Purl 2 rows.

Row 3: (K2tog, k3) to end (24 sts).

Row 4: Purl.

Row 5: (K2tog, k1) to end (16 sts).

Row 6: (P2tog) to end (8 sts).

Break yarn and thread through sts on needle, pull tight and secure by threading yarn a second time through sts.

EYES (make 2)

Using the long tail method and yarn F, cast on 16 sts.

Row 1: (P2tog) to end (8 sts).

Break yarn and thread through sts on needle, pull tight and secure by threading yarn a second time through sts.

BEAK

Using the long tail method and yarn D, cast on 11 sts.

Row 1: Purl.

Row 2: K2tog, k to last 2 sts, k2tog (9 sts).

Row 3: P2tog, p to last 2 sts, p2tog (7 sts).

Row 4: As row 2 (5 sts).

Row 5: Purl.

Break yarn and thread through sts on needle, pull tight and secure by threading yarn a second time through sts.

BRACES (make 2)

Using the long tail method and yarn E, cast on 44 sts.

Row 1: Knit.

Cast off kwise.

MAKING UP

Note: Sew up all row-end seams on right side using mattress stitch one stitch in from the edge, unless otherwise stated; a one-stitch seam allowance has been allowed for this.

BODY AND HEAD

Sew up side edges, and with this seam at centre back, sew across top of head. Stuff head and body pushing stuffing into ears. Sew across lower edge.

TUMMY

Place tummy on Owl on row above waist and sew along outside edge.

LEGS

Sew up side edges of legs and stuff. Pin legs to body leaving a ¾in (2cm) gap at crotch and sew in place.

TROUSERS

Place two pieces of trousers together matching all edges and sew up inside leg seams and across crotch. Sew up side seams and place trousers on Owl. Sew cast-off stitches of waist of trousers to row above waist of Owl using backstitch.

FEET AND TOES

Sew up side edges of back toe of foot and stuff back toe with a tiny bit of stuffing with tweezers or tip of scissors. Finish sewing up side edges and place inside a triangle of thick cardboard measuring 1in (2.5cm) on short edge and 1¼in (3cm) on long sides. Oversew cast-on stitches enclosing cardboard inside. Sew up side edges of each toe and sew a toe to middle of each foot and two more either side at front. Sew feet to ends of legs.

WINGS

Sew up side edges of wings and with this seam at centre of inside edge, pin and sew wings to Owl at both sides.

EYE PATCHES, EYES AND BEAK

Place eye patches side by side and join. Pin eye patches to Owl and sew around outside edge. Sew row ends of eyes together and sew eyes to centre of eye patches. Sew up side edges of beak and stuff beak with tweezers or tip of scissors. With seam at centre of back edge, sew across top of beak. Sew beak to Owl.

BRACES AND BUTTONS

Sew ends of braces to top edge of trousers, take braces over shoulders, cross over and sew to back of trousers. Sew braces to body down centre of braces. Add two buttons to front of trousers.

WILD BOAR

INFORMATION YOU'LL NEED

MATERIALS
Any DK (US: light worsted) yarn
(amounts given are approximate)
Yarn A ginger (20g for each Wild Boar)
Yarn B dark brown (10g)
Yarn C orange (15g)
Yarn D yellow (15g)
Yarn E cream (5g)
Oddment of black for embroidery and dark
brown for making up
1 pair of 3.25mm (UK10:US3) needles and
a spare needle of same size for dungarees
Knitters' pins and a blunt-ended needle for
sewing up
Acrylic toy stuffing
2 small buttons for each wild boar

FINISHED SIZE
Wild Boar stands 7½in (19cm) tall

TENSION
26 sts x 34 rows measure 4in (10cm)
square over st-st using 3.25mm needles
and DK yarn before stuffing.

ABBREVIATIONS
See page 156

HOW TO MAKE WILD BOAR

BODY

Using the long tail method and yarn A, cast on 44 sts.

Row 1: Purl.

Row 2: K1, (k10, m1, k1, m1, k10) twice, k1 (48 sts).

Rows 3 to 9: Work 7 rows in st-st.

Rows 10 and 11: Work 2 rows in g-st to mark waist.

Rows 12 to 15: Beg with a k row, work 4 rows in st-st.

Row 16: K1, (k10, k3tog, k10) twice, k1 (44 sts).

Rows 17 to 19: Work 3 rows in st-st.

Row 20: K1, (k9, k3tog, k9) twice, k1 (40 sts).

Rows 21 to 23: Work 3 rows in st-st.

Row 24: K1, (k8, k3tog, k8) twice, k1 (36 sts).

Row 25: Purl.

Cast off.

HEAD

Using the long tail method and yarn A, cast on 36 sts.

Row 1 and foll alt row: Purl.

Row 2: (K8, m1, k2, m1, k8) twice (40 sts).

Rows 3 to 17: Work 15 rows in st-st.

Row 18: (K2tog, k3) to end (32 sts).

Row 19 and foll 2 alt rows: Purl.

Row 20: (K2tog, k2) to end (24 sts).

Row 22: (K2tog, k1) to end (16 sts).

Row 24: (K2tog) to end (8 sts).
Break yarn and thread through sts on needle, pull tight and secure by threading yarn a second time through sts.

SNOUT

Using the long tail method and yarn A, cast on 9 sts.

Row 1: Purl.

Row 2: (Kfb) to end (18 sts).

Rows 3 to 5: P 3 rows.

Rows 6 to 9: Beg with a k row, work 4 rows in st-st.

Row 10: K3, (m1, k4) 3 times, m1, k3 (22 sts).

Rows 11 to 13: Work 3 rows in st-st.

Row 14: K5, (m1, k4) 3 times, m1, k5 (26 sts).

Row 15: Purl.

Cast off.

TROTTERS AND LEGS
(make 2)
Using the long tail method and yarn B, cast on 7 sts.

Row 1 and foll alt row: Purl.
Row 2: (Kfb) to end (14 sts).
Row 4: (Kfb, k1) to end (21 sts).
Rows 5 to 9: Work 5 rows in st-st. Change to yarn A and dec:
Row 10: (K2tog, k1) to end (14 sts).
Rows 11 to 21: Work 11 rows in st-st.
Cast off.

TROTTERS AND FOREARMS (make 2)
Using the long tail method and yarn B, cast on 8 sts.

Row 1: Purl.
Row 2: (Kfb) to end (16 sts).
Rows 3 to 7: Work 5 rows in st-st. Change to yarn A and dec:
Row 8: (K2tog, k2) to end (12 sts).
Rows 9 to 21: Work 13 rows in st-st.
Row 22: (K2tog, k1) to end (8 sts). Break yarn, thread through sts on needle and leave loose.

DUNGAREES
(make 2 pieces)
Note: foll individual instructions as given for 1 front and 1 back of dungarees.

FIRST LEG
Using the long tail method and yarn C, cast on 12 sts and beg in g-st.

Rows 1 and 2: Work 2 rows in g-st.
Break yarn and set aside.

SECOND LEG
Work as for first leg but do not break yarn.

JOIN LEGS
Row 3: Beg with second leg and k10, k2tog, turn, using the knitting-on method cast on 5 sts, turn, then with the same yarn continue across first leg and k2tog, k to end (27 sts).
Row 4 and foll 2 alt rows: Purl.
Row 5: (K2, m1) twice, k19, (m1, k2) twice (31 sts).
Row 7: (K2, m1) twice, k9, k2tog, k1, k2tog, k9, (m1, k2) twice (33 sts).
Row 9: K13, k2tog, k3, k2tog, k13 (31 sts).
Rows 10 to 14: Work 5 rows in st-st.
Rows 15 to 17: Work 3 rows in g-st, ending with a RS row. Cast off in g-st for back of dungarees or cont with bib for front of dungarees:

DIVIDE FOR BIB
Row 18: Cast off 9 sts kwise, k12

(13 sts now on RH needle), cast off rem 9 sts and fasten off. Rejoin yarn to rem sts and patt:
Row 19: K2, (k1 tbl) 9 times, k2 (13 sts).
Row 20: K2, p9, k2.
Row 21: Knit.
Rows 22 to 27: Rep rows 20 and 21, 3 times more, ending with a k row.
Rows 28 and 29: Work 2 rows in g-st, ending with a RS row.
Cast off in g-st.

STRAPS FOR DUNGAREES (make 2)
Using the long tail method and yarn C, cast on 30 sts.
Row 1: Knit.
Cast off kwise.

PINAFORE
Using the long tail method and yarn D, cast on 81 sts and beg in g-st.
Rows 1 and 2: Work 2 rows in g-st.
Rows 3 to 14: Beg with a k row, work 12 rows in st-st.
Row 15: K1, (k2tog, k2) to end (61 sts).

Rows 16 and 17: Work 2 rows in g-st, ending with a RS row.
DIVIDE FOR BIB
Row 18: Cast off 24 sts kwise, k12 (13 sts now on RH needle) cast off rem 24 sts and fasten off. Rejoin yarn to rem sts and work bib from **, as for dungarees.

STRAPS FOR PINAFORE (make 2)
Using yarn D make straps, as for dungarees.

EARS (make 2)
Using the long tail method and yarn B, cast on 10 sts.
Row 1: Purl.
Row 2: (Kfb) to end (20 sts).
Rows 3 to 13: Work 11 rows in st-st.
Row 14: K2tog, (k4, k2tog) to end (16 sts).
Row 15: Purl.
Row 16: (K2tog) to end (8 sts).
Rows 17 to 19: Work 3 rows in st-st.
Row 20: (K2tog) to end (4 sts).
Break yarn and thread through sts on needle, pull tight and secure by threading yarn a second time through sts.

TAIL

Using the long tail method and yarn A, cast on 15 sts.
Cast off kwise.

TUSKS FOR BUCK (make 2)

Using the long tail method and yarn E, cast on 9 sts.
Rows 1 to 5: Beg with a p row, work 5 rows in st-st.
Row 6: (K2tog, k1) to end (6 sts). Break yarn and thread through sts on needle, pull tight and secure by threading yarn a second time through sts.

MAKING UP

Note: Sew up all row-end seams on right side using mattress stitch one stitch in from the edge, unless otherwise stated; a one-stitch seam allowance has been allowed for this.

BODY

Sew up side edges of body and with this seam at centre back, oversew cast-on stitches. Stuff body and leave neck open.

HEAD AND SNOUT

Sew up side edges of head and stuff. Sew lower edge of head to body, making a horizontal stitch over one stitch from head, then a horizontal stitch over one stitch from body, and do this alternately all the way round. Sew up side edges of snout and stuff. Pin and sew snout to Wild Boar.

TROTTERS AND LEGS

Gather round cast-on stitches of trotters, pull tight and secure. Sew up side edges of trotters and legs and stuff. Pin legs to body leaving a ¾in (2cm) gap at crotch and sew in place. Shape trotters using dark brown and embroider a loop around centre of trotters, pull tight, then go a second time around and secure.

TROTTERS AND FOREARMS

Gather round cast-on stitches of trotters, pull tight and secure. Sew up side edges of trotters and forearms, stuff, and pull stitches on a thread tight and secure. Sew forearms to Wild Boar at each side. Shape trotters as for legs.

DUNGAREES, STRAPS AND BUTTONS

Make up dungarees, straps and buttons, as for Deer on page 22.

PINAFORE, STRAPS AND BUTTONS

Make up pinafore, straps and buttons, as for Deer on page 22.

EARS

Sew up side edges of ears and press flat. Sew ears to back of head, curl tips forward and sew in place.

FEATURES

Mark position of eyes with two pins above snout and embroider eyes in black, making a vertical chain stitch for each eye, then a second chain stitch on top of first. Embroider eyebrows and nostrils in black, using straight stitches for eyebrows and long chain stitches for nostrils (see page 155 for how to begin and fasten off invisibly for the embroidery).

TAIL

Fold over tip of tail and sew in place. Position tail at rear of Wild Boar below waistband and sew in place.

TUSKS FOR BUCK

Roll up tusks from row ends to row ends and sew in place. Sew tusks to sides of snout.

BEAVER

INFORMATION YOU'LL NEED

MATERIALS

Any DK (US: light worsted) yarn (amounts given are approximate)

Yarn A brown (20g for each beaver)

Yarn B teal (15g)

Yarn C dark brown (15g)

Yarn D charcoal (20g)

Yarn E rose pink (15g)

Yarn F white (5g)

Yarn G oatmeal (5g)

Yarn H black (2g)

Oddment of black for embroidery

1 pair of 3.25mm (UK10:US3) needles

Knitters' pins and a blunt-ended needle for sewing up

Tweezers (optional)

Acrylic toy stuffing

2 small buttons for each beaver

FINISHED SIZE

Beaver stands 7in (18cm) tall

TENSION

26 sts x 34 rows measure 4in (10cm) square over st-st using 3.25mm needles and DK yarn before stuffing.

ABBREVIATIONS

See page 156

HOW TO MAKE BEAVER

BODY AND HEAD

Using the long tail method and yarn A, cast on 8 sts.

Row 1 and foll 4 alt rows: Purl.

Row 2: (Kfb) to end (16 sts).

Row 4: (Kfb, k1) to end (24 sts).

Row 6: (Kfb, k2) to end (32 sts).

Row 8: (Kfb, k3) to end (40 sts).

Row 10: (Kfb, k4) to end (48 sts).

Rows 11 to 21: Work 11 rows in st-st.

Rows 22 and 23: Work 2 rows in g-st to mark waist.

Rows 24 to 39: Beg with a k row, work 16 rows in st-st.

Row 40: K21, (m1, k1) 7 times, k20 (55 sts).

Row 41 and foll 2 alt rows: Purl.

Row 42: K26 (m1, k1) 4 times, k25 (59 sts).

Row 44: (K2, k2tog) twice, k43, (k2tog, k2) twice (55 sts).

Row 46: k2tog, k to last 2 sts, k2tog (53 sts).

Row 47: Purl.

Rows 48 to 53: Rep rows 46 and 47, 3 times more (47 sts).

Row 54: K2tog, k17, (k2tog) twice, k1, (k2tog) twice, k17, k2tog (41 sts).

Row 55: P18, p2tog, p1, p2tog, p18 (39 sts).

Row 56: K2tog, k13, (k2tog) twice, k1, (k2tog) twice, k13, k2tog (33 sts).

Row 57: P2tog, p12, p2tog, p1, p2tog, p12, p2tog (29 sts).

Row 58: (K2tog) twice, k6, (k2tog) twice, k1, (k2tog) twice, k6, (K2tog) twice (21 sts).

Row 59: P2tog, p6, p2tog, p1, p2tog, p6, p2tog (17 sts). Cast off.

DUNGAREES

Using the long tail method and yarn B, cast on 8 sts.

Row 1 and foll 5 alt rows: Purl.

Row 2: (Kfb) to end (16 sts).

Row 4: As row 2 (32 sts).

Row 6: (Kfb, k3) to end (40 sts).

Row 8: (Kfb, k4) to end (48 sts).

Row 10: (Kfb, k5) to end (56 sts).

Row 12: (Kfb, k6) to end (64 sts).

Rows 13 to 23: Beg with a p row, work 11 rows in st-st.

Rows 24 to 26: Work 3 rows in g-st, ending with a RS row.

**DIVIDE FOR BIB

Row 27: Cast off 25 sts kwise, k13 (14 sts now on RH needle), cast off rem 25 sts kwise and fasten off.

Rejoin yarn to rem sts and patt:

Row 28: K2, (k1 tbl) 10 times, k2 (14 sts).

Row 29: K2, p10, k2.

Row 30: Knit.

Rows 31 to 36: Rep rows 29 and 30, 3 times more, ending with a k row.

Rows 37 and 38: Work 2 rows in g-st, ending with a RS row. Cast off in g-st.

FEET (make 2)

Using the long tail method and yarn C, cast on 26 sts.

Row 1 and foll alt row: Purl.

Row 2: K2, m1, k8, (m1, k2) 4 times, k6, m1, k2 (32 sts).

Row 4: K2, m1, k11, (m1, k2) 4 times, k9, m1, k2 (38 sts).

Rows 5 to 11: Work 7 rows in st-st.

Row 12: K2, k2tog, k11, (k2tog) 4 times, k11, k2tog, k2 (32 sts).

Row 13: Purl.

Row 14: K2, k2tog, k8, (k2tog) 4 times, k8, k2tog, k2 (26 sts). Cast off pwise.

TAIL (make 2 pieces)

Using the long tail method and yarn D, cast on 10 sts and work in g-st.

Rows 1 and 2: Work 2 rows in g-st.

Row 3: K1, m1, k to last st, m1, k1 (12 sts).

Rows 4 to 6: Work 3 rows in g-st.

Rows 7 to 26: Rep rows 3 to 6, 5 times more (22 sts).

Rows 27 to 36: Work 10 rows in g-st.

Row 37: K2tog, k to last 2 sts, k2tog (20 sts).

Row 38 to 40: Work 3 rows in g-st.

Row 41: K2tog, k to last 2 sts, k2tog (18 sts).

Row 42: Knit.

Rows 43 to 48: Rep rows 41 and 42, 3 times more (12 sts).

Rows 49 and 51: Rep row 41, 3 times more (6 sts).

Cast off in g-st.

PINAFORE

Using the long tail method and yarn E, cast on 85 sts and beg in g-st.

Rows 1 and 2: Work 2 rows in g-st.

Rows 3 to 14: Beg with a k row, work 12 rows in st-st.

Row 15: K1, (k2tog, k2) to end (64 sts).

Rows 16 and 17: Work 2 rows in g-st, ending with a RS row.

DIVIDE FOR BIB

Work from ** to end, as for dungarees.

FOREARMS AND PAWS (make 2)

Using the long tail method and yarn A, cast on 10 sts.

Rows 1 to 13: Beg with a p row, work 13 rows in st-st. Change to yarn C and inc:

Row 14: K2, (m1, k2) to end (14 sts).

Rows 15 to 19: Work 5 rows in st-st.

Row 20: K1, (k2tog) to last st, k1 (8 sts).

Break yarn and thread through sts on needle, pull tight and secure by threading yarn a second time through sts.

STRAPS FOR DUNGAREES (make 2)

Using the long tail method and yarn B, cast on 36 sts.

Row 1: Knit.

Cast off kwise.

STRAPS FOR PINAFORE (make 2)

Using yarn E make straps, as for dungarees.

TEETH

Using the long tail method and yarn F, cast on 11 sts.

Row 1: P5, k1, p5.

Row 2: K5, p1, k5.

Rows 3 to 7: Rep rows 1 and 2 twice more, then row 1 once.

Cast off kwise.

SNOUT (make 2 pieces)

Using the long tail method and yarn G, cast on 16 sts.

Rows 1 to 3: Beg with a p row, work 3 rows in st-st.

Row 4: (K2tog) to end (8 sts). Break yarn and thread through sts on needle, pull tight and secure by threading yarn a second time through sts.

NOSE

Using the long tail method and yarn H, cast on 10 sts.

Row 1: Purl.

Row 2: K1, (k2tog, k1) to end (7 sts).

Break yarn and thread through sts on needle, pull tight and secure by threading yarn a second time through sts.

EARS (make 2)

Using the long tail method and yarn C, cast on 16 sts.

Rows 1 to 3: Beg with a p row, work 3 rows in st-st.

Row 4: (K2tog) to end (8 sts). Break yarn and thread through sts on needle, pull tight and secure by threading yarn a second time through sts.

MAKING UP

Note: Sew up all row-end seams on right side using mattress stitch one stitch in from the edge, unless otherwise stated; a one-stitch seam allowance has been allowed for this.

BODY AND HEAD

Gather round cast-on stitches, pull tight and secure. Fold cast-off stitches in half and oversew. Sew up side edges of body leaving a gap, stuff and sew up gap.

DUNGAREES

Gather round cast-on stitches, pull tight and secure. Sew up side edges from stitches pulled tight on a thread to waist and place dungarees on Beaver. Sew cast-off stitches of waist of dungarees to row above waist using backstitch.

FEET

Fold cast-off stitches in half and oversew. Fold cast-on stitches in half and oversew. Stuff feet and sew up side edges. Place feet side by side and sew heels together. Sew feet to underneath of Beavers, sewing through dungarees to body, or sew feet to body for Beaver in pinafore.

TAIL

Place wrong sides of two pieces of tail together, matching all edges and oversew around outside edge. Sew tail to back of Beaver.

PINAFORE

Sew up side edges of skirt of pinafore and place pinafore on Beaver over head. Sew cast-off stitches of waist of pinafore to row above waist using backstitch.

PAWS AND FOREARMS

Sew up side edges of paws and stuff paws. Sew up arms and stuff with tweezers or tip of scissors. Gather round cast-on stitches of forearms, pull tight and secure. Sew forearms to Beaver in a forwards position at each side.

STRAPS AND BUTTONS

Sew ends of straps to top edge of front of bib, take straps over shoulders, cross over and sew to back of dungarees or pinafore. Add two buttons to bib.

TEETH, SNOUT AND NOSE

Fold outside edges of teeth to centre of back and sew in position. Sew teeth to head. Sew up row ends of two pieces of snout and place side by side and sew together where they meet. Place a tiny ball of stuffing into each half, pin and sew snout to front of head over teeth. Sew up side edges of nose and sew nose above snout in middle.

FEATURES

Mark position of eyes with two pins and embroider eyes in black making a vertical chain stitch for each eye, then a second chain stitch on top of first. Embroider eyebrows in black using straight stitches (see page 155 for how to begin and fasten off invisibly for the embroidery).

EARS

Sew up side edges of ears, press flat. Position ears and pin and sew ears to head.

RACOON

INFORMATION YOU'LL NEED

MATERIALS
Any DK (US: light worsted) yarn
(amounts given are approximate)
Yarn A grey (15g)
Yarn B black (5g)
Yarn C cream (15g)
Yarn D dark brown (15g)
Yarn E amethyst (10g)
Oddment of black for embroidery
1 pair of 3.25mm (UK10:US3)
needles and a spare needle of
same size
Knitters' pins and a blunt-ended
needle for sewing up
Acrylic toy stuffing
2 small buttons

FINISHED SIZE
Racoon stands 7½in (19cm) tall

TENSION
26 sts x 34 rows measure 4in (10cm)
square over st-st using 3.25mm
needles and DK yarn before stuffing.

ABBREVIATIONS
See page 156

HOW TO MAKE RACOON

BODY
Using the long tail method and yarn A, cast on 36 sts.
Row 1: Purl.
Row 2: K1, (k8, m1, k1, m1, k8) twice, k1 (40 sts).
Rows 3 to 9: Work 7 rows in st-st.
Rows 10 and 11: Work 2 rows in g-st to mark waist.
Rows 12 to 19: Beg with a k row, work 8 rows in st-st.
Row 20: K1, (k8, k3tog, k8) twice, k1 (36 sts).
Row 21 and foll 2 alt rows: Purl.
Row 22: K1, (k7, k3tog, k7) twice, k1 (32 sts).
Row 24: K1, (k6, k3tog, k6) twice, k1 (28 sts).
Row 26: K1, (k5, k3tog, k5) twice, k1 (24 sts).
Row 27: Purl.
Cast off.

HEAD
Using the long tail method and yarn B, cast on 7 sts.
Row 1: Purl.
Row 2: K1, (kfb, k1) to end (10 sts).
Row 3: Purl.
Join on yarns A, C and D and work in colours, carrying yarns C and D behind yarn A.
Row 4: Yarn C-p4, yarn A-p2, yarn C-p4.
Row 5: Yarn C-k2, (m1, k1) twice, yarn A-k2, yarn C-(k1, m1) twice, k2 (14 sts).

Row 6: Yarn C-p6, yarn A-p2, yarn C-p6.
Row 7: Yarn C-(k1, m1) 4 times, k2, yarn A-k2, yarn C-k2, (m1, k1) 4 times (22 sts).
Row 8: Yarn C-p10, yarn A-p2, yarn C-p10.
Row 9: Yarn C-(k2, m1) 4 times, k2, yarn A-k2, yarn C-(k2, m1) 4 times, k2 (30 sts).
Row 10: Yarn D-p14, yarn A-p2, yarn D-p14.
Row 11: Yarn D-k4, (m1, k2) 4 times, k2, yarn A-k1, m1, k1, yarn D-k4, (m1, k2) 4 times, k2 (39 sts).
Row 12: Yarn D-p18, yarn A-p3, yarn D-p18.
Row 13: Yarn D-k6, (m1, k2) 4 times, k4, yarn A-k3, yarn D-k6, (m1, k2) 4 times, k4 (47 sts).
Row 14: Yarn D-p22, yarn A-p3, yarn D-p22.
Row 15: Yarn D-k22, yarn A-k3, yarn D-k22.
Row 16: As row 14.
Row 17: Yarn C-k22, yarn A-k3, yarn C-k22.
Row 18: Yarn C-p22, yarn A-p3, yarn C-p22.
Rows 19 to 26: Rejoin yarn A and cont in yarn A and work 8 rows in st-st.
Row 27: K8, (k2tog, k1) 3 times, k14, (k2tog, k1) 3 times, k7 (41 sts).
Row 28 and foll alt row: Purl.

Row 29: K7, (k2tog, k1) 3 times, k10, (k2tog, k1) 3 times, k6 (35 sts).
Row 31: K4, (k2tog, k1) 4 times, k4, (k2tog, k1) 4 times, k3 (27 sts).
Row 32: Purl.
Cast off.

FEET AND LEGS (make 2)
Using the long tail method and yarn D, cast on 8 sts.
Row 1 and foll alt row: Purl.
Row 2: (Kfb) to end (16 sts).
Row 4: (Kfb, k1) to end (24 sts).
Rows 5 to 9: Work 5 rows in st-st.
Change to yarn A and dec:
Row 10: (K2tog, k1) to end (16 sts).
Rows 11 to 21: Work 11 rows in st-st.
Cast off.

PAWS AND FOREARMS (make 2)
Using the long tail method and yarn D, cast on 9 sts.
Row 1: Purl.
Row 2: (Kfb) to end (18 sts).
Rows 3 to 7: Work 5 rows in st-st.
Change to yarn A and dec:
Row 8: (K2tog, k1) to end (12 sts).
Rows 9 to 21: Work 13 rows in st-st.
Row 22: (K2tog, k1) to end (8 sts).
Break yarn, thread through sts on needle and leave loose.

DUNGAREES AND STRAPS

Work dungarees and straps using yarn E, as for Badger on page 27.

EARS (make 2)

Note: Make 2 pieces in yarn A and 2 pieces in yarn C.

Using the long tail method and yarn A or C, cast on 9 sts.

Row 1 and foll 2 alt rows: Purl.
Row 2: K3, k3tog, k3 (7 sts).
Row 4: K2, k3tog, k2 (5 sts).
Row 6: K1, k3tog, k1 (3 sts).
Row 7: P3tog tbl (1 st).
Fasten off.

TAIL

Using the long tail method and yarn D, cast on 10 sts and work in g-st.

Row 1: Knit.
Row 2: (Kfb) to end (20 sts).
Rows 3 to 10: Work 8 rows in g-st.
Rows 11 to 18: Join on yarn C and work 8 rows in g-st.
Rows 19 to 26: Using yarn D, work 8 rows in g-st.
Rows 27 to 34: Using yarn C, work 8 rows in g-st.

Rows 35 to 74: Rep rows 19 to 34, twice more, then rows 19 to 26 once.
Cont in yarn D and dec:
Row 75: (K2tog, k2) to end (15 sts).
Row 76: Knit.
Row 77: (K2tog, k1) to end (10 sts).
Row 78: Knit.
Break yarn and thread through sts on needle, pull tight and secure by threading yarn a second time through sts.

MAKING UP

Note: Sew up all row-end seams on right side using mattress stitch one stitch in from the edge, unless otherwise stated; a one-stitch seam allowance has been allowed for this.

BODY

Sew up side edges of body and with this seam at centre back, oversew cast-on stitches. Stuff body leaving neck open.

HEAD

Weave in ends around intarsia. Gather round cast-on stitches, pull tight and secure. Sew up side edges leaving a gap, and with this seam at centre of underneath sew across cast-off stitches. Stuff, pushing stuffing into nose and sew up gap. Pin and sew head to body making a short stitch from head, then a short stitch from body, and do this alternately all the way round.

FEET AND LEGS

Gather round cast-on stitches of feet, pull tight and secure. Sew up side edges of feet and legs, stuff feet then stuff legs. Pin legs to body leaving a ¾in (2cm) gap at crotch and sew in place.

PAWS AND FOREARMS

Gather round cast-on stitches of forearms, pull tight and secure. Sew up side edges, stuff paws and forearms and pull stitches on a thread tight and secure. Sew forearms to Racoon at each side.

DUNGAREES, STRAPS AND BUTTONS

Make up dungarees, straps and buttons, as for Deer on page 22.

EARS

Place two pieces of ears, one grey and one cream together, wrong sides together and sew around outside edge. Repeat for other ear, position ears and pin and sew ears to head.

TAIL

Sew up side edges of tail, stuffing as you sew. Sew tail to back of Racoon.

FEATURES

Mark position of eyes with two pins and embroider eyes in grey making a vertical chain stitch for each eye, then a second chain stitch on top of first. Embroider eyebrows in grey using straight stitches (see page 155 for how to begin and fasten off invisibly for the embroidery).

HEDGEHOG

INFORMATION YOU'LL NEED

MATERIALS
Any DK (US: light worsted) yarn
(amounts given are approximate)
Yarn A pale brown (25g)
Yarn B dark brown (20g)
Yarn C black (2g)
Yarn D dark green (10g)
Oddment of black for embroidery
1 pair of 3.25mm (UK10:US3) needles and
a spare needle of same size
3 knitters' bobbins
Knitters' pins and a blunt-ended
needle for sewing up
Acrylic toy stuffing
2 small buttons

FINISHED SIZE
Hedgehog stands 6¾in (17cm) tall

TENSION
26 sts x 34 rows measure 4in (10cm) square
over st-st using 3.25mm needles and DK
yarn before stuffing.

ABBREVIATIONS
See page 156

Special abbreviation
w1: wrap 1 stitch – take yarn between
needles to opposite side, slip 1 stitch pwise
from LH needle to RH needle, then take
yarn between needles to first side.

HOW TO MAKE HEDGEHOG

LOWER BODY AND FRONT

Using the long tail method and yarn A, cast on 36 sts.

Row 1: Purl.

Row 2: K1, (k8, m1, k1, m1, k8) twice, k1 (40 sts).

Rows 3 to 11: Work 9 rows in st-st.

Rows 12 and 13: Work 2 rows in g-st to mark waist.

Row 14: Cast off 12 sts, k15 (16 sts now on RH needle), cast off rem 12 sts and fasten off (16 sts).

WORK FRONT

Rows 15 to 23: Rejoin yarn to rem sts and beg with a p row, work 9 rows in st-st.

Row 24: K2tog, k to last 2 sts, k2tog (14 sts).

Row 25: Purl.

Row 26: As row 24 (12 sts).

Row 27: Purl.

Cast off.

BACK OF BODY

Using the long tail method and yarn A, cast on 20 sts loosely. Join on yarn B and work in yarn A and yarn B held together, treated as 1 strand.

Row 1: Knit.

Row 2: K1, *k next st placing index finger of LH behind RH needle and wind yarn round finger and needle clockwise once, then wind just round needle in the same direction once, k st pulling 2 loops through, place these loops on LH needle and k into the back of them, pull on loop just made to secure (this will be referred to as loop-st); rep from * 17 times more, k1.

Row 3: Knit.

Row 4: K1, (loop-st) to last st, k1.

Rows 5 to 12: Rep rows 3 and 4, 4 times more.

Row 13: K1, (k2tog, k2) to last 3 sts, k2tog, k1 (15 sts).

Row 14: K1, (loop-st) to last st, k1.

Cast off.

HEAD AND SNOUT

Using the long tail method and yarn C, cast on 8 sts and beg in rev st-st.

Rows 1 to 3: Beg with a p row, work 3 rows in rev st-st.

Row 4: Change to yarn A and p 1 row.

Row 5: (K1, m1) twice, k4, (m1, k1) twice (12 sts).

Row 6: Purl.

Row 7: (K1, m1) twice, k3, m1, k2, m1, k3, (m1, k1) twice (18 sts).

Rows 8 to 10: Work 3 rows in st-st.

Row 11: (K1, m1) twice, k6, m1, k2, m1, k6, (m1, k1) twice (24 sts).

Row 12: Purl.

Row 13: (K1, m1) twice, k9, m1, k2, m1, k9, (m1, k1) twice (30 sts).

Rows 14 to 18: Work 5 rows in st-st.

Join on yarn B and work with yarn A and yarn B together, treating them as one strand.

Row 19: Knit.

Row 20: K5, *k next st placing index finger of LH behind RH needle and wind yarn round finger and needle clockwise once, then wind just round needle in the same direction once, k st pulling 2 loops through, place these loops on LH needle and k into the back of them, pull on loop just made to secure (this will be referred to as loop-st); rep from * 19 times more, k5.

Row 21: K22, w1 (see special abbreviation), turn.

Row 22: S1p, (loop-st) 14 times, w1.

Row 23: S1p, k to end.

Row 24: K5, (loop-st) 20 times, k5.

Rows 25 to 28: Rep rows 21 to 24 once.

Row 29: K2, (k2tog, k2) to end (23 sts).

Row 30: K4, (loop-st) 15 times, k4.

Row 31: K2tog, (k1, k2tog) to end (15 sts).

Row 32: K3, (loop-st) 9 times, k3.
Row 33: K2, (k2tog, k1) 4 times, k1 (11 sts).
Row 34: K2, (loop-st) 7, k2.
Row 35: K2tog, (k1, k2tog) to end (7 sts).
Row 36: K1, (loop-st) 5 times, k1.
Break yarn and thread through sts on needle, pull tight and secure by threading yarn a second time through sts.

FEET AND LEGS (make 2)

Using the long tail method and yarn A, cast on 16 sts.
Row 1: Purl.
Row 2: (K1, kfb) 4 times, (kfb, k1) 4 times (24 sts).
Rows 3 to 9: Work 7 rows in st-st.
Row 10: K4, (k2tog) 8 times, k4 (16 sts).
Rows 11 to 13: Work 3 rows in st-st.
Cast off.

PAWS AND FOREARMS
(make 2)

Using the long tail method and yarn A, cast on 8 sts.
Row 1: Purl.
Row 2: (Kfb) to end (16 sts).
Rows 3 to 7: Work 5 rows in st-st.
Row 8: (K2tog, k2) to end (12 sts).
Rows 9 to 17: Work 9 rows in st-st.
Row 18: (K2tog, k1) to end (8 sts).
Break yarn, thread through sts on needle and leave loose.

DUNGAREES
(make 2 pieces)

Note: foll individual instructions as given for 1 front and 1 back of dungarees.

FIRST LEG

Using the long tail method and yarn D, cast on 12 sts and beg in g-st.
Rows 1 and 2: Work 2 rows in g-st.
Break yarn and set aside.

SECOND LEG

Work as for first leg but do not break yarn.

JOIN LEGS

Row 3: Beg with second leg and k10, k2tog, turn, using the knitting-on method cast on 5 sts, turn, then with the same yarn continue across first leg and k2tog, k to end (27 sts).
Row 4 and foll 2 alt rows: Purl.
Row 5: K2, m1, k23, m1, k2 (29 sts).
Row 7: K12, k2tog, k1, k2tog, k12 (27 sts).
Row 9: K10, k2tog, k3, k2tog, k10 (25 sts).
Rows 10 to 16: Work 7 rows in st-st.
Rows 17 to 19: Work 3 rows in g-st, ending with a RS row.
Cast off in g-st for back of dungarees or cont with bib for front of dungarees:

DIVIDE FOR BIB

Row 20: Cast off 7 sts kwise, k10

(11 sts now on RH needle), cast off rem 7 sts and fasten off. Rejoin yarn to rem sts and patt:
Row 21: K2, (k1 tbl) 7 times, k2 (11 sts).
Row 22: K2, p7, k2.
Row 23: Knit.
Rows 24 to 29: Rep rows 22 and 23, 3 times more, ending with a k row.
Rows 30 and 31: Work 2 rows in g-st, ending with a RS row.
Cast off in g-st.

STRAPS FOR DUNGAREES
(make 2)

Using the long tail method and yarn D, cast on 30 sts.
Row 1: Knit.
Cast off kwise.

EARS (make 2)

Using the long tail method and yarn A, cast on 8 sts.
Row 1: Purl.
Row 2: (K1, m1) 3 times, k2, (m1, k1) 3 times (14 sts).
Rows 3 to 6: Work 4 rows in st-st, ending on a k row.
Row 7: P2, (p2tog, p2) to end (11 sts).
Break yarn and thread through sts on needle, pull tight and secure by threading yarn a second time through sts.

MAKING UP

Note: Sew up all row-end seams on right side using mattress stitch one stitch in from the edge, unless otherwise stated; a one-stitch seam allowance has been allowed for this.

LOWER BODY, FRONT AND BACK OF BODY

Sew up side edges of lower body. Sew lower edge of back of body to cast-off stitches of lower body. Sew up sides then oversew across cast-on stitches of lower body. Stuff body leaving neck open.

HEAD AND SNOUT

Gather round cast-on stitches of snout, pull tight and secure. Sew up side edges of snout and stuff head and snout. Gather round row ends of head, pull tight and secure. Pin and sew head to body by making a horizontal stitch from head, then a horizontal stitch from body and do this alternately all the way round.

FEET AND LEGS

Fold cast-on stitches of feet in half and oversew. Sew up side edges of feet and legs and stuff. Pin legs to body leaving a ¾in (2cm) gap at crotch and sew in place.

PAWS AND FOREARMS

Gather round cast-on stitches of paws, pull tight and secure. Sew up side edges of paws and place a small ball of stuffing into paws. Sew up side edges of arms, stuff, and pull stitches on a thread tight and secure. Sew forearms to body of Hedgehog at each side.

DUNGAREES, STRAPS AND BUTTONS

Make up dungarees, straps and buttons, as for Deer on page 22.

EARS

Sew up side edges of ears and with this seam at centre back, press flat. Position ears among prickles and pin and sew ears to head.

FEATURES

Mark position of eyes with two pins and embroider eyes in black making a vertical chain stitch for each eye, then a second chain stitch on top of first. Embroider eyebrows in black using long stitches (see page 155 for how to begin and fasten off invisibly for the embroidery).

CUCKOO

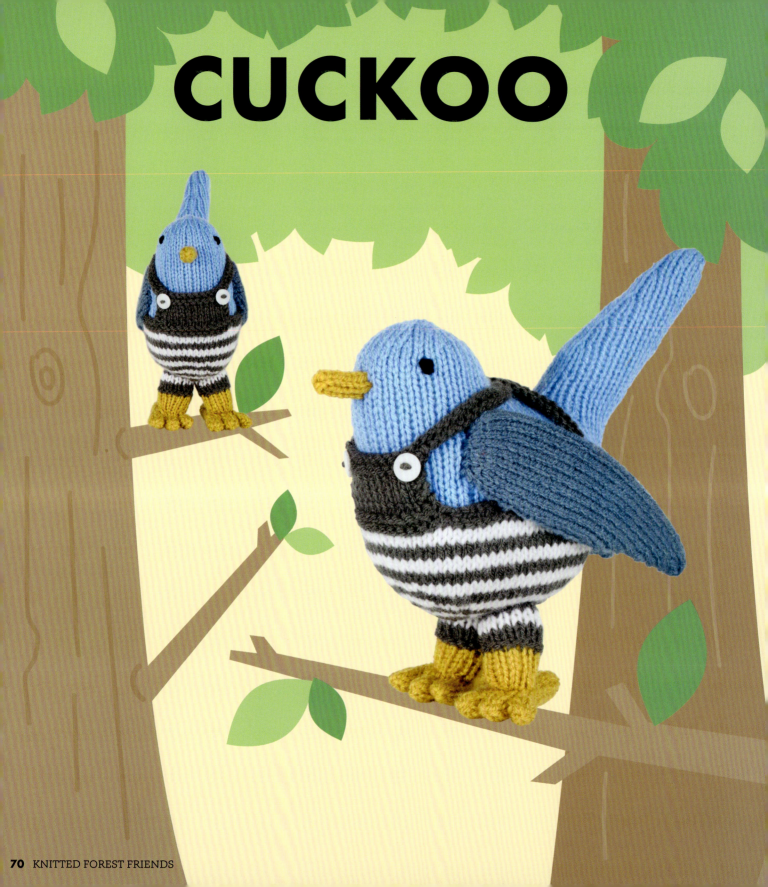

INFORMATION YOU'LL NEED

MATERIALS
Any DK (US: light worsted) yarn
(amounts given are approximate)
Yarn A light blue (20g)
Yarn B dark grey (10g)
Yarn C white (10g)
Yarn D yellow (5g)
Yarn E pale denim (10g)
Oddment of black for embroidery
1 pair of 3.25mm (UK10:US3) needles
Knitters' pins and a blunt-ended needle for sewing up
Tweezers (optional)
Acrylic toy stuffing
1 chenille stem
2 small buttons

FINISHED SIZE
Cuckoo stands 8in (20.5cm) tall

TENSION
26 sts x 34 rows measure 4in (10cm) square over st-st
using 3.25mm needles and DK yarn before stuffing.

ABBREVIATIONS
See page 156

Special abbreviation
w1: wrap 1 stitch – take yarn between needles to
opposite side, slip 1 stitch pwise from LH needle to
RH needle, then take yarn between needles to first side.

HOW TO MAKE CUCKOO

BODY, HEAD AND TAIL

Using the long tail method and yarn A, cast on 22 sts.

Row 1 and foll 5 alt rows: Purl.

Row 2: K2, (m1, k2) to end (32 sts).

Row 4: *(K2, m1) twice, k8, (m1, k2) twice; rep from * once (40 sts).

Row 6: *(K2, m1) twice, k12, (m1, k2) twice; rep from * once (48 sts).

Row 8: *K2, m1, k20, m1, k2; rep from * once (52 sts).

Row 10: *K2, m1, k22, m1, k2; rep from * once (56 sts).

Row 12: *K2, m1, k24, m1, k2; rep from * once (60 sts).

Rows 13 to 19: Work 7 rows in st-st.

Rows 20 and 21: Work 2 rows in g-st to mark waist.

Rows 22 to 25: Work 4 rows in st-st.

Row 26: K56, w1 (see special abbreviation), turn.

Row 27: S1p, p52, w1, turn.

Row 28: S1k, k to end.

Row 29: P54, w1, turn.

Row 30: S1k, k48, w1, turn.

Row 31: S1p, p to end.

Row 32: K52, w1, turn.

Row 33: S1p, p44, w1, turn.

Row 34: S1k, k to end.

Row 35: P50, w1, turn.

Row 36: S1k, k40, w1, turn.

Row 37: S1p, p to end.

Row 38: K10, cast off 3 sts, k33, turn.

Row 39: P34, turn and work on these 34 sts.

Row 40: k2tog, k to last 2 sts, k2tog (32 sts).

Rows 41 to 47: Work 7 rows in st-st.

Row 48: (K2tog, k2) to end (24 sts).

Row 49 and foll alt row: Purl.

Row 50: (K2tog, k1) to end (16 sts).

Row 52: (K2tog) to end (8 sts). Break yarn and thread through sts on needle, pull tight and secure by threading yarn a second time through sts.

Row 53: Rejoin yarn to rem sts halfway along row, cast off 3 sts, k to end.

Row 54: Push rem sts together and p 1 row (20 sts).

Rows 55 to 64: Work 10 rows in st-st.

Row 65: K8, (k2tog) twice, k8 (18 sts).

Rows 66 to 70: Work 5 rows in st-st.

Row 71: K7, (k2tog) twice, k7 (16 sts).

Rows 72 to 76: Work 5 rows in st-st.

Row 77: K6, (k2tog) twice, k6 (14 sts).

Rows 78 to 82: Work 5 rows in st-st.

Row 83: K5, (k2tog) twice, k5 (12 sts).

Rows 84 to 90: Work 7 rows in st-st.
Cast off.

DUNGAREES
(make 2 pieces)

Using the long tail method and yarn B, cast on 22 sts.

Row 1: Purl.

Row 2: K2, (m1, k2) to end (32 sts).

Row 3: Purl.

Join on yarn C and work in stripes carrying yarn loosely up side of work.

Row 4: Yarn C-*(K2, m1) twice, k8, (m1, k2) twice; rep from * once (40 sts).

Row 5: Yarn C-purl.

Row 6: Yarn B-*(K2, m1) twice, k12, (m1, k2) twice; rep from * once (48 sts).

Row 7: Yarn B-purl.

Row 8: Yarn C-*(K2, m1) twice, k16, (m1, k2) twice; rep from * once (56 sts).

Row 9: Yarn C-purl.

Row 10: Yarn B-*(K2, m1) twice, k20, (m1, k2) twice; rep from * once (64 sts).

Row 11: Yarn B-purl.

Row 12: Yarn C-*K2, m1, k28, m1, k2; rep from * once (68 sts).

Row 13: Yarn C-purl.

Row 14: Yarn B-*K2, m1, k30, m1, k2; rep from * once (72 sts).

Row 15: Yarn B-purl.
Rows 16 to 21: Work 6 rows in st-st stripes as set.
Rows 22 to 24: Cont in yarn B and work 3 rows in g-st, ending with a RS row.

DIVIDE FOR BIB

Row 25: Cast off 29 sts kwise, k13 (14 sts now on RH needle), cast off rem 29 sts and fasten off. Rejoin yarn B to rem sts and patt:
Row 26: K2, (k1 tbl) 10 times, k2 (14 sts).
Row 27: K2, p10, k2.
Row 28: Knit.
Rows 29 to 32: Rep rows 27 and 28, twice more, ending with a k row.
Rows 33 and 34: Work 2 rows in g-st, ending with a RS row.
Cast off in g-st.

STRAPS FOR DUNGAREES (make 2)

Using the long tail method and yarn B, cast on 32 sts.
Row 1: Knit.
Cast off kwise.

LEGS (make 2)

Using the long tail method and yarn D, cast on 7 sts.
Row 1: Purl.
Row 2: (Kfb) to end (14 sts).
Rows 3 to 7: Work 5 rows in st-st.
Row 8: Change to yarn B and k 1 row.
Row 9: K4, (kfb, k4) twice (16 sts).

Rows 10 and 11: K 1 row then p 1 row.
Rows 12 and 13: Join on yarn C and k 1 row then p 1 row.
Rows 14 and 15: Yarn B-k 1 row then p 1 row.
Cast off in yarn B.

FEET AND BACK TOE, AND TOES

Make feet and back toe, and toes in yarn D, as for Owl on page 39.

WINGS (make 2)

Using the long tail method and yarn E, cast on 14 sts.
Row 1: Purl.
Row 2: K2, (m1, k2) to end (20 sts).
Rows 3 to 27: Beg with a p row, work 25 rows in st-st.
Row 28: K2tog, k to last 2 sts, k2tog (18 sts).
Rows 29 to 31: Work 3 rows in st-st.
Rows 32 to 47: Rep rows 28 to 31, 4 times more (10 sts).
Row 48: (k2tog) to end (5 sts).
Break yarn and thread through sts on needle, pull tight and secure by threading yarn a second time through sts.

BEAK

Using the long tail method and yarn D, cast on 7 sts.
Rows 1 to 7: Beg with a p row, work 7 rows in st-st.
Break yarn and thread through sts on needle, pull tight and secure by threading yarn a second time through sts.

MAKING UP

Note: Sew up all row-end seams on right side using mattress stitch one stitch in from the edge, unless otherwise stated; a one-stitch seam allowance has been allowed for this.

BODY, HEAD AND TAIL

Sew up side edges of head, sew across back and side edges, down to cast-on stitches. Stuff head and body. Fold cast-on stitches in half and oversew.

DUNGAREES, STRAPS AND BUTTONS

Sew up side edges of dungarees and place on cuckoo. Sew waist of dungarees to waist of Cuckoo using backstitch all the way round. Sew ends of straps to bib, take straps over shoulders, cross over and sew to sides. Add two buttons to bib.

LEGS

Sew up side edges of legs and stuff legs. Sew legs to underneath of Cuckoo, sewing through dungarees to body.

FEET AND TOES

Make up feet and toes as for Owl on page 40 and sew to legs.

WINGS

Fold wings and oversew open edges. Pin and sew wings to Cuckoo at each side.

BEAK

Fold chenille stem in half and place fold into wrong side of stitches pulled tight on a thread. Sew up side edges of beak enclosing chenille stem inside. Cut excess chenille stem and sew beak to head.

FEATURES

Mark position of eyes with two pins and embroider eyes in black making a vertical chain stitch for each eye, then a second chain stitch on top of first (see page 155 for how to begin and fasten off invisibly for the embroidery).

ANT

INFORMATION YOU'LL NEED

MATERIALS

Any DK (US: light worsted) yarn
(amounts given are approximate)
Yarn A brown (20g)
Yarn B blue (5g)
Yarn C sapphire blue (5g)
Oddment of black for embroidery
and brown for making up
1 pair of 3.25mm (UK10:US3)
needles and a spare needle of
same size
3 knitters' bobbins
Knitters' pins and a blunt-ended
needle for sewing up
Acrylic toy stuffing
14 chenille stems
2 small buttons

FINISHED SIZE

Ant stands 8¾in (22cm) tall

TENSION

26 sts x 34 rows measure 4in (10cm)
square over st-st using 3.25mm
needles and DK yarn before stuffing.

ABBREVIATIONS

See page 156

HOW TO MAKE ANT

BODY

Using the long tail method and yarn A, cast on 8 sts.

Row 1 and foll 4 alt rows: Purl.

Row 2: (Kfb) to end (16 sts).

Row 4: (Kfb, k1) to end (24 sts).

Row 6: (Kfb, k2) to end (32 sts).

Row 8: (Kfb, k3) to end (40 sts).

Row 10: (Kfb, k4) to end (48 sts).

Rows 11 to 13: Work 3 rows in st-st.

Rows 14 and 15: Work 2 rows in g-st to mark waist.

Rows 16 to 23: Beg with a k row, work 8 rows in st-st.

Row 24: (K2tog, k2) to end (36 sts).

Place a marker on last row for middle gathering and keep on RS.

Rows 25 to 31: Work 7 rows in st-st.

Row 32: (K2tog, k2) to end (27 sts).

Row 33: Purl.

Row 34: (K2tog, k1) to end (18 sts).

Row 35: Purl.

Cast off.

HEAD

Using the long tail method and yarn A, cast on 9 sts.

Row 1 and foll 2 alt rows: Purl.

Row 2: (Kfb) to end (18 sts).

Row 4: (Kfb, k1) to end (27 sts).

Row 6: (Kfb, k2) to end (36 sts).

Rows 7 to 17: Work 11 rows in st-st.

Row 18: (K2tog, k2) to end (27 sts).

Rows 19 to 21: Work 3 rows in st-st.

Row 22: (K2tog, k1) to end (18 sts).

Rows 23 to 25: Work 3 rows in st-st.

Row 26: (K2tog) to end (9 sts). Break yarn and thread through sts on needle, pull tight and secure by threading yarn a second time through sts.

LEGS AND FEET (make 2)

Using the long tail method and yarn A, cast on 11 sts.

Rows 1 to 13: Beg with a p row, work 13 rows in st-st.

Row 14: K2, (m1, k1) to last st, k1 (19 sts).

Rows 15 to 19: Work 5 rows in st-st.

Row 20: K1, (k2tog, k1) to end (13 sts).

Row 21: Purl.

Row 22: K1, (k2tog, k1) to end (9 sts).

Break yarn and thread through sts on needle, pull tight and secure by threading yarn a second time through sts.

ARMS AND PAWS
(make 2)

Using the long tail method and yarn A, cast on 11 sts.

Rows 1 to 15: Beg with a p row, work 15 rows in st-st.

Row 16: K4, (m1, k1) 4 times, k3 (15 sts).

Rows 17 to 21: Work 5 rows in st-st.

Row 22: (K2tog, k1) to end (10 sts).

Row 23: Purl.

Row 24: (K2tog) to end (5 sts). Break yarn and thread through sts on needle, pull tight and secure by threading yarn a second time through sts.

TROUSERS (make 2 pieces)
FIRST LEG

Using the long tail method and yarn B, cast on 8 sts and beg in g-st.

Rows 1 and 2: Work 2 rows in g-st.

Break yarn and set aside.

SECOND LEG

Work as for first leg but do not break yarn.

JOIN LEGS

Row 3: Beg with second leg and k6, k2tog, turn, using the knitting-on method, cast on 5 sts, turn, then with the same yarn continue across first leg and k2tog, k to end (19 sts).

Row 4 and foll 3 alt rows: Purl.

Row 5: K2, m1, k to last 2 sts, m1, k2 (21 sts).

Row 7: (K2, m1) twice, k4, k2tog, k1, k2tog, k4, (m1, k2) twice (23 sts).

Row 9: K2, m1, k to last 2 sts, m1, k2 (25 sts).

Row 11: K2, m1, k7, k2tog, k3, k2tog, k7, m1, k2 (25 sts).

Rows 12 to 16: Work 5 rows in st-st.

Rows 17 to 19: Work 3 rows in g-st, ending with a RS row. Cast off in g-st.

BRACES (make 2)

Using the long tail method and yarn C, cast on 34 sts.

Row 1: Knit.

Cast off kwise.

ANTENNAE (make 2)

Using the long tail method and yarn A, cast on 7 sts.

Rows 1 to 7: Beg with a p row, work 7 rows in st-st.

Row 8: K1, (m1, k1) to end (13 sts).

Rows 9 to 11: Work 3 rows in st-st.

Row 12: K1, (k2tog, k1) to end (9 sts). Break yarn and thread through sts on needle, pull tight and secure by threading yarn a second time through sts.

MAKING UP

Note: Sew up all row-end seams on right side using mattress stitch one stitch in from the edge, unless otherwise stated; a one-stitch seam allowance has been allowed for this.

BODY
Gather round cast-on stitches, pull tight and secure. Sew up side edges of body and stuff body leaving neck open. Shape upper body segment with a double length of brown yarn and sew a running stitch around row with marker on, sewing in and out of every half stitch. Pull yarn in and knot yarn, sewing ends into body.

HEAD
Gather round cast-on stitches of head, pull tight and secure. Sew up row ends leaving a gap, stuff head and sew up gap. Pin and sew head to body.

LEGS AND FEET
Sew up side edges of feet. Take three chenille stems together and fold in half. Place fold into feet and stuff feet. Sew up legs enclosing chenille stems inside. Cut excess chenille stems and pin and sew legs to body leaving a ¾in (2cm) gap at crotch.

ARMS AND PAWS
Sew up side edges of paws. Take three chenille stems together and fold in half. Place fold into paws and stuff paws. Sew up arms enclosing chenille stems inside. Cut excess chenille stems and gather round cast-on stitches, pull tight and secure. Pin and sew arms to body with shoulders halfway down upper body section.

TROUSERS, BRACES AND BUTTONS
Place two pieces of trousers together matching all edges, sew up inside leg seams and across crotch. Sew up side seams and place trousers on Ant. Sew trousers to row above waist of Ant using backstitch all the way round. Sew ends of straps to front of trousers, take straps over shoulders, cross over and sew to back waist. Add two buttons to front of trousers.

ANTENNAE
Fold a chenille stem in half and place fold on wrong side of stitches pulled tight on a thread. Sew up side edges of antennae enclosing chenille stem inside. Cut excess chenille stem and sew antennae to top of head.

FEATURES
Mark position of eyes with two pins and embroider eyes in black making a ring of chain stitches and fill in ring with more chain stitches. Embroider eyebrows and mouth using straight stitches (see page 155 for how to begin and fasten off invisibly for the embroidery).

BEAR

INFORMATION YOU'LL NEED

MATERIALS
Any DK (US: light worsted) yarn (amounts given are approximate)
Yarn A brown (20g for each Bear)
Yarn B pale brown (5g)
Yarn C sapphire blue (10g)
Yarn D dusky pink (10g)
Oddment of black for embroidery
1 pair of 3.25mm (UK10:US3) needles and a spare needle of same size for dungarees
Knitters' pins and a blunt-ended needle for sewing up
Acrylic toy stuffing
2 small buttons for each Bear

FINISHED SIZE
Bear stands 7½in (19cm) tall

TENSION
26 sts x 34 rows measure 4in (10cm) square over st-st using 3.25mm needles and DK yarn before stuffing.

ABBREVIATIONS
See page 156

HOW TO MAKE BEAR

BODY

Using the long tail method and yarn A, cast on 36 sts.

Row 1: Purl.

Row 2: K1, (k8, m1, k1, m1, k8) twice, k1 (40 sts).

Rows 3 to 11: Work 9 rows in st-st.

Rows 12 and 13: Work 2 rows in g-st to mark waist.

Rows 14 to 25: Work 12 rows in st-st.

Row 26: K1, (k8, k3tog, k8) twice, k1 (36 sts).

Row 27 and foll alt row: Purl.

Row 28: K1, (k7, k3tog, k7) twice, k1 (32 sts).

Row 30: K1, (k6, k3tog, k6) twice, k1 (28 sts).

Row 31: Purl.

Cast off.

HEAD

Using the long tail method and yarn A, cast on 28 sts.

Row 1: Purl.

Row 2: K3, (m1, k2) to last st, k1 (40 sts).

Rows 3 to 15: Work 13 rows in st-st.

Row 16: (K2tog, k3) to end (32 sts).

Row 17 and foll 2 alt rows: Purl.

Row 18: (K2tog, k2) to end (24 sts).

Row 20: (K2tog, k1) to end (16 sts).

Row 22: (K2tog) to end (8 sts). Break yarn and thread through sts on needle, pull tight and secure by threading yarn a second time through sts.

SNOUT

Using the long tail method and yarn B, cast on 16 sts.

Rows 1 to 3: Beg with a p row, work 3 rows in st-st.

Row 4: K2tog, k to last 2 sts, k2tog (14 sts).

Row 5: P2tog, p to last 2 sts, p2tog (12 sts).

Row 6: (K2tog) to end (6 sts). Break yarn and thread through sts on needle, pull tight and secure by threading yarn a second time through sts.

FEET AND LEGS (make 2)

Using the long tail method and yarn A, cast on 15 sts.

Row 1: Purl.

Row 2: (Kfb) to end (30 sts).

Rows 3 to 9: Work 7 rows in st-st.

Row 10: K7, (k2tog) 8 times, k7 (22 sts).

Row 11: Purl.

Row 12: K5, (k2tog) 6 times, k5 (16 sts).

Rows 13 to 19: Work 7 rows in st-st.

Cast off.

PAWS AND FOREARMS
(make 2)

Using the long tail method and yarn A, cast on 10 sts.

Row 1: Purl.

Row 2: (Kfb) to end (20 sts).

Rows 3 to 7: Work 5 rows in st-st.

Row 8: (K2tog, k2) to end (15 sts).

Rows 9 to 23: Work 15 rows in st-st.

Row 24: (K2tog, k1) to end (10 sts). Break yarn, thread through sts on needle and leave loose.

DUNGAREES
(make 2 pieces)

Note: foll individual instructions as given for 1 front and 1 back of dungarees.

FIRST LEG

Using the long tail method and yarn C, cast on 12 sts and beg in g-st.

Rows 1 and 2: Work 2 rows in g-st.

Rows 3 and 4: K 1 row then p 1 row.

Break yarn and set aside.

SECOND LEG

Work as for first leg but do not break yarn.

JOIN LEGS

Row 5: Beg with second leg and k10, k2tog, turn, using the knitting-on method, cast on 5 sts, turn, then with the same yarn continue across first leg and k2tog, k to end (27 sts).

Row 6 and foll 2 alt rows: Purl.

Row 7: K2, m1, k23, m1, k2 (29 sts).

Row 9: K12, k2tog, k1, k2tog, k12 (27 sts).

Row 11: K10, k2tog, k3, k2tog, k10 (25 sts).

Rows 12 to 18: Work 7 rows in st-st.

Rows 19 to 21: Work 3 rows in g-st, ending with a RS row.

Cast off in g-st for back of dungarees or cont with bib for front of dungarees:

DIVIDE FOR BIB

Row 22: Cast off 7 sts kwise, k10 (11 sts now on RH needle), cast off rem 7 sts and fasten off. Rejoin yarn to rem sts and patt:

**Row 23: K2, (k1 tbl) 7 times, k2 (11 sts).

Row 24: K2, p7, k2.

Row 25: Knit.

Rows 26 to 33: Rep rows 24 and 25, 4 times more, ending with a k row.

Rows 34 and 35: Work 2 rows in g-st, ending with a RS row.

Cast off in g-st.

STRAPS FOR DUNGAREES (make 2)

Using the long tail method and yarn C, cast on 28 sts.

Row 1: Knit.

Cast off kwise.

PINAFORE

Using the long tail method and yarn D, cast on 65 sts and beg in g-st.

Rows 1 and 2: Work 2 rows in g-st.

Rows 3 to 16: Beg with a k row, work 14 rows in st-st.

Row 17: K1, (k2tog, k2) to end (49 sts).

Rows 18 and 19: Work 2 rows in g-st, ending with a RS row.

DIVIDE FOR BIB

Row 20: Cast off 19 sts kwise, k10 (11 sts now on RH needle), cast off rem 19 sts and fasten off. Rejoin yarn to rem sts and work bib from **, as for dungarees.

STRAPS FOR PINAFORE (make 2)

Make straps for pinafore using yarn D, as for dungarees.

EARS (make 2)

Using the long tail method and yarn A, cast on 16 sts.

Rows 1 to 5: Work 5 rows in st-st.

Row 6: K1, (k2tog, k1) to end (11 sts).

Break yarn and thread through sts on needle, pull tight and secure by threading yarn a second time through sts.

MAKING UP

Note: Sew up all row-end seams on right side using mattress stitch one stitch in from the edge, unless otherwise stated; a one-stitch seam allowance has been allowed for this.

BODY

Sew up side edges of body and with this seam at centre back, oversew cast-on stitches. Stuff body leaving neck open.

HEAD AND SNOUT

Sew up side edges of head and Stuff. Pin and sew head to body by making a horizontal stitch over one stitch from head, then a horizontal stitch over one stitch from body and do this alternately all the way round. Sew up side edges of snout and stuff. Pin and sew snout to head all the way round.

FEET AND LEGS

Fold cast-on stitches of feet in half and oversew. Sew up side edges of legs and stuff feet and legs. Pin legs to body leaving a ¾in (2cm) gap at crotch and sew in place.

PAWS AND FOREARMS

Gather round cast-on stitches of forearms, pull tight and secure. Sew up side edges of forearms and stuff. Pull stitches on a thread tight and secure. Sew forearms to Bear at each side.

DUNGAREES, STRAPS AND BUTTONS

Make up dungarees, straps and buttons, as for Deer on page 22.

PINAFORE, STRAPS AND BUTTONS

Make up pinafore, straps and buttons, as for Deer on page 22.

EARS

Sew up side edges of ears and with seam at centre back, press flat. Position ears and pin and sew ears to head.

FEATURES

Mark position of eyes with two pins and embroider eyes in black making a vertical chain stitch for each eye, then a second chain stitch on top of first. Embroider eyebrows in black using straight stitches. Embroider nose on snout in black using satin stitch and a vertical long stitch (see page 155 for how to begin and fasten off invisibly for the embroidery).

KOALA

INFORMATION YOU'LL NEED

MATERIALS
Any DK (US: light worsted) yarn
(amounts given are approximate)
Yarn A grey (25g) **NOTE: 2 separate balls
of Yarn A are required**
Yarn B white (10g)
Yarn C grass green (10g)
Yarn D dark green (5g)
Yarn E charcoal (5g)
Oddment of black for embroidery
1 pair of 3.25mm (UK10:US3) needles and
a spare needle of same size
Knitters' pins and a blunt-ended needle for
sewing up
Acrylic toy stuffing
Tweezers (optional)
2 small buttons

FINISHED SIZE
Koala stands 7½in (19cm) tall

TENSION
26 sts x 34 rows measure 4in (10cm) square
over st-st using 3.25mm needles and DK
yarn before stuffing.

ABBREVIATIONS
See page 156

HOW TO MAKE KOALA

BODY
Using the long tail method and yarn A, cast on 36 sts.
Row 1: Purl.
Row 2: K1, (k8, m1, k1, m1, k8) twice, k1 (40 sts).
Rows 3 to 9: Work 7 rows in st-st.
Rows 10 and 11: Work 2 rows in g-st to mark waist.
Join on yarn B and second ball of yarn A and work in intarsia, twisting yarn when changing colours to avoid a hole.
Row 12: Yarn A-k14, yarn B-k12, yarn A (second ball)-k14.
Row 13: Yarn A-p14, yarn B-p12, yarn A-p14.
Rows 14 to 17: Rep rows 12 and 13, twice more.
Row 18: Yarn A-k15, yarn B-k10, yarn A-k15.
Row 19: Yarn A-p15, yarn B-p10, yarn A-p15.
Row 20: Yarn A-k9, k3tog, k4, yarn B-k8, Yarn A-k4, k3tog, k9 (36 sts).
Row 21: Yarn A-p14, yarn B-p8, yarn A-p14.
Row 22: Yarn A-k8, k3tog, k4, yarn B-k6, Yarn A-k4, k3tog, k8 (32 sts).

Row 23: Yarn A-p14, yarn B-p4, yarn A-p14.
Cont in yarn A and dec:
Row 24: K1, (k6, k3tog, k6) twice, k1 (28 sts).
Row 25: Purl.
Cast off.

HEAD
Using the long tail method and yarn A, cast on 28 sts.
Row 1: Purl.
Row 2: K3, (m1, k1) 10 times, k3, (m1, k1) 10 times, k2 (48 sts).
Rows 3 to 19: Work 17 rows in st-st.
Row 20: K4, (k2tog, k1) 6 times, k5, (k2tog, k1) 6 times, k3 (36 sts).
Row 21: Purl.
Row 22: K4, (k2tog) 6 times, k4, (k2tog) 6 times, k4 (24 sts).
Row 23: Purl.
Cast off.

FEET AND LEGS (make 2)
Using the long tail method and yarn A, cast on 15 sts.
Row 1: Purl.
Row 2: (Kfb) to end (30 sts).
Rows 3 to 9: Work 7 rows in st-st.

Row 10: K7, (k2tog) 8 times, k7 (22 sts).
Row 11: Purl.
Row 12: K5, (k2tog) 6 times, k5 (16 sts).
Rows 13 to 19: Work 7 rows in st-st.
Cast off.

PAWS AND FOREARMS (make 2)
Using the long tail method and yarn A, cast on 8 sts.
Row 1 and foll alt row: Purl.
Row 2: (Kfb) to end (16 sts).
Row 4: (Kfb, k3) to end (20 sts).
Rows 5 to 9: Work 5 rows in st-st.
Row 10: (K2tog, k2) to end (15 sts).
Rows 11 to 23: Work 13 rows in st-st.
Row 24: (K2tog, k1) to end (10 sts).
Break yarn, thread through sts on needle and leave loose.

TROUSERS (make 2 pieces)
FIRST LEG
Using the long tail method and yarn C, cast on 12 sts and beg in g-st.

Rows 1 and 2: Work 2 rows in g-st.

Rows 3 and 4: K 1 row then p 1 row.

Break yarn and set aside.

SECOND LEG

Work as for first leg but do not break yarn.

JOIN LEGS

Row 5: Beg with second leg and k10, k2tog, turn, using the knitting-on method cast on 5 sts, turn, then with the same yarn continue across first leg and k2tog, k to end (27 sts).

Row 6 and foll 2 alt rows: Purl.

Row 7: K2, m1, k23, m1, k2 (29 sts).

Row 9: K12, k2tog, k1, k2tog, k12 (27 sts).

Row 11: K10, k2tog, k3, k2tog, k10 (25 sts).

Rows 12 to 16: Work 5 rows in st-st.

Rows 17 to 19: Work 3 rows in g-st, ending with a RS row. Cast off in g-st.

BRACES (make 2)

Using the long tail method and yarn D, cast on 32 sts.

Row 1: Knit.

Cast off kwise.

NOSE

Using the long tail method and yarn E, cast on 5 sts and work in g-st.

Row 1: Kfb, k3, kfb (7 sts).

Rows 2 to 11: Work 10 rows in g-st.

Row 12: K2tog, k3, k2tog (5 sts).

Row 13: K2tog, k1, k2tog (3 sts). Cast off.

EARS (make 4 pieces)

Using the long tail method and yarn B, cast on 24 sts.

Row 1: Purl.

Row 2: k5, (k2tog, k4) 3 times, k1 (21 sts).

Row 3: Change to yarn A and p 1 row.

Row 4: K2, (k2tog, k3) 3 times, k2tog, k2 (17 sts).

Row 5 and foll alt row: Purl.

Row 6: K2tog, (k1, k2tog) to end (11 sts).

Row 8: K2tog, (k1, k2tog) to end (7 sts).

Break yarn and thread through sts on needle, pull tight and secure by threading yarn a second time through sts.

MAKING UP

Note: Sew up all row-end seams on right side using mattress stitch one stitch in from the edge, unless otherwise stated; a one-stitch seam allowance has been allowed for this.

BODY

Sew up side edges of body and with this seam at centre back, oversew cast-on stitches. Stuff body leaving neck open.

HEAD

Sew up side edges of head and with this seam at centre back, sew across cast-off stitches. Stuff, then pin and sew head to body by making a horizontal stitch over one stitch from head, then a horizontal stitch over one stitch from body and do this alternately all the way round.

FEET AND LEGS

Fold cast-on stitches of feet in half and oversew. Sew up side edges of legs and stuff feet and legs. Pin legs to body leaving a ¾in (2cm) gap at crotch and sew in place.

PAWS AND FOREARMS

Gather round cast-on stitches of forearms, pull tight and secure. Sew up side edges of forearms and stuff. Pull stitches on a thread tight and secure. Sew forearms to Koala at each side.

TROUSERS, BRACES AND BUTTONS

Place two pieces of trousers together matching all edges and sew up inside leg seams and across crotch. Sew up side seams and place trousers on Koala. Sew cast-off stitches of waist of trousers to row above waist of Koala using backstitch. Sew ends of braces to top edge of trousers at front, take straps over shoulders, cross over and sew to back of trousers. Add two buttons to front of trousers.

NOSE

Place nose on head and pin and sew nose to head using backstitch around outside edge leaving a gap.

Stuff with a little stuffing using tweezers or tip of scissors, then sew up gap.

EARS

Place two sides of each ear together, right sides outside and oversew around cast-on stitches. Position ears and pin and sew ears to head.

FEATURES

Mark position of eyes with two pins and embroider eyes in black making a vertical chain stitch for each eye, then a second chain stitch on top of first. Embroider eyebrows in black using straight stitches (see page 155 for how to begin and fasten off invisibly for the embroidery).

GIANT PANDA

INFORMATION YOU'LL NEED

MATERIALS
Any DK (US: light worsted) yarn
(amounts given are approximate)
Yarn A white (20g)
Yarn B black (20g)
Yarn C red (10g)
Yarn D grey (5g)
Oddments of black and white for embroidery
1 pair of 3.25mm (UK10:US3) needles and a
spare needle of same size
Knitters' pins and a blunt-ended needle for
sewing up
Acrylic toy stuffing
2 small buttons

FINISHED SIZE
Giant Panda measures 8in (20.5cm) tall

TENSION
26 sts x 34 rows measure 4in (10cm) square over
st-st using 3.25mm needles and DK yarn before
stuffing.

ABBREVIATIONS
See page 156

SPECIAL ABBREVIATION
w1: wrap 1 stitch – take yarn between needles to
opposite side, slip 1 stitch pwise from LH needle
to RH needle, then take yarn between needles to
first side.

HOW TO MAKE GIANT PANDA

BODY

Using the long tail method and yarn A, cast on 44 sts.

Row 1: Purl.

Row 2: K1, (k10, m1, k1, m1, k10) twice, k1 (48 sts).

Rows 3 to 9: Work 7 rows in st-st.

Rows 10 and 11: Work 2 rows in g-st to mark waist.

Rows 12 to 17: Beg with a k row, work 6 rows in st-st.

Row 18: K1, (k10, k3tog, k10) twice, k1 (44 sts).

Row 19: Purl.

Rows 20 to 21: Change to yarn B and work 2 rows in st-st.

Row 22: K1, (k9, k3tog, k9) twice, k1 (40 sts).

Rows 23 to 25: Work 3 rows in st-st.

Row 26: K1, (k8, k3tog, k8) twice, k1 (36 sts).

Rows 27: Purl.

Cast off.

HEAD

Using the long tail method and yarn A, cast on 36 sts.

Row 1: Purl.

Row 2: *K4, (m1, k2) 6 times, k2; rep from * once (48 sts).

Rows 3 to 19: Work 17 rows in st-st

Row 20: (K2tog, k4) to end (40 sts).

Row 21 and foll 3 alt rows: Purl.

Row 22: (K2tog, k3) to end (32 sts).

Row 24: (K2tog, k2) to end (24 sts).

Row 26: (K2tog, k1) to end (16 sts).

Row 28: (K2tog) to end (8 sts).

Break yarn and thread through sts on needle, pull tight and secure by threading yarn a second time through sts.

FEET AND LEGS (make 2)

Using the long tail method and yarn B, cast on 16 sts.

Row 1 and foll alt row: Purl.

Row 2: *K1, (kfb) twice, k1; rep from * 3 times more (24 sts).

Row 4: *K2, (kfb) twice, k2; rep from * 3 times more (32 sts).

Rows 5 to 9: Work 5 rows in st-st.

Row 10: K8, (k2tog) 8 times, k8 (24 sts).

Rows 11 to 19: Work 9 rows in st-st.

Cast off.

PAWS AND ARMS (make 2)

Using the long tail method and yarn B, cast on 10 sts.

Row 1: Purl.

Row 2: (Kfb) to end (20 sts).

Rows 3 to 7: Work 5 rows in st-st.

Row 8: K16, w1 (see special abbreviation), turn.

Row 9: S1p, p12, w1 turn.

Row 10: S1k, k to end.

Row 11: Purl.

Rows 12 to 15: Rep rows 8 to 11 once.

Row 16: (K2tog) twice, k2, (kfb, k1) twice, (k1, kfb) twice, k2, (k2tog) twice (20 sts).

Row 17: Purl.

Rows 18 to 25: Rep rows 8 to 11 twice more.

Row 26: K2tog, (k1, k2tog) to end (13 sts).

Row 27: Purl.

Row 28: K1, (k2tog, k1) to end (9 sts).

Break yarn and thread through sts on needle, pull tight and secure by threading yarn a second time through sts.

TROUSERS (make 2 pieces)

FIRST LEG

Using the long tail method and yarn C, cast on 16 sts and beg in g-st.

Rows 1 and 2: Work 2 rows in g-st.

Break yarn and set aside.

SECOND LEG

Work as for first leg but do not break yarn.

JOIN LEGS

Row 3: Beg with second leg and k14, k2tog, turn, using the knitting-on method cast on 5 sts, turn, then with the same yarn continue across first leg and k2tog, k to end (35 sts).

Rows 4 to 6: Beg with a p row, work 3 rows in st-st.

Row 7: K15, k2tog, k1, k2tog, k15 (33 sts).

Row 8: Purl.
Row 9: K13, k2tog, k3, k2tog, k13 (31 sts).
Rows 10 to 14: Work 5 rows in st-st.
Rows 15 to 17: Work 3 rows in g-st ending with a RS row. Cast off in g-st.

BRACES (make 2)

Using the long tail method and yarn D, cast on 36 sts.
Row 1: Knit.
Cast off kwise.

SNOUT

Using the long tail method and yarn A, cast on 24 sts.
Rows 1 to 5: Beg with a p row, work 5 rows in st-st.
Row 6: (K2tog, k1) to end (16 sts).
Row 7: Purl.
Row 8: (K2tog) to end (8 sts).
Break yarn and thread through sts on needle, pull tight and secure by threading yarn a second time through sts.

EYE PIECES (make 2)

Using the long tail method and yarn B, cast on 24 sts.
Row 1: Purl.
Row 2: (K2tog) twice, k4, (k2tog) 4 times, k4, (k2tog) twice (16 sts).
Row 3: P1, p2tog, p2, (p2tog) 3 times, p2, p2tog, p1 (11 sts)
Cast off.

EARS (make 2)

Using the long tail method and yarn B, cast on 14 sts.
Row 1: Purl.
Row 2: k2, (m1, K2) to end (20 sts).
Rows 3 to 7: Work 5 rows in st-st.
Row 8: (K2tog, k2) to end (15 sts).
Row 9: Purl.
Row 10: (K2tog, k1) to end (10 sts).
Break yarn and thread through sts on needle, pull tight and secure by threading yarn a second time through sts.

MAKING UP

Note: Sew up all row-end seams on right side using mattress stitch one stitch in from the edge, unless otherwise stated; a one-stitch seam allowance has been allowed for this.

BODY

Sew up side edges of body and with this seam at centre back, oversew cast-on stitches. stuff body leaving neck open.

HEAD

Sew up side edges of head and stuff. Pin and sew head to body, making a horizontal stitch over one stitch from head, then a horizontal stitch over one stitch from body, and do this alternately all the way round.

FEET AND LEGS

Fold cast-on stitches of feet in half and oversew. Sew up side edges of legs and stuff feet and legs. Pin legs to body leaving a ¾in (2cm) gap at crotch and sew in place.

PAWS AND ARMS

Gather round cast-on stitches, pull tight and secure. Sew up side edges of arms leaving a gap, stuff and sew up gap. Pin and sew arms to Giant Panda at each side.

TROUSERS, BRACES AND BUTTONS

Place two pieces of trousers together matching all edges and sew up inside leg seams and across crotch. Sew up side seams and place trousers on Giant Panda. Sew cast-off stitches of waist of trousers to row above waist of Giant Panda using back-stitch. Sew ends of braces to top edge of trousers at front, take straps over shoulders, cross over and sew to back of trousers. Add two buttons to front of trousers.

SNOUT

Sew up side edges of snout and stuff. Pin and sew snout to Giant Panda.

EYE PIECES

Fold cast-off stitches in half, oversew and sew up row ends. Position eye patches on head and sew around outer edge using backstitch.

EARS

Sew up side edges of ears and with this seam at centre back, position ears and pin and sew ears to Giant Panda.

FEATURES

Mark position of eyes with two pins and embroider eyes in white making a ring of chain stitches for each eye. Embroider nose and mouth in black using satin stitch for nose and straight stitches for mouth (see page 155 for how to begin and fasten off invisibly for the embroidery).

WOODPECKER

INFORMATION YOU'LL NEED

MATERIALS
Any DK (US: light worsted) yarn
(amounts given are approximate)
Yarn A black (15g)
Yarn B white (5g)
Yarn C red (5g)
Yarn D denim (10g)
Yarn E grey (5g)
Oddment of black for embroidery
1 pair of 3.25mm (UK10:US3) needles
Knitters' pins and a blunt-ended needle for sewing up
Tweezers (optional)
Acrylic toy stuffing
Thick cardboard, approximately 3 x 1½in (7.5 x 4cm)
1 chenille stem
2 small buttons

FINISHED SIZE
Woodpecker stands 7¼in (18.5cm) tall

TENSION
26 sts x 34 rows measure 4in (10cm) square over st-st using 3.25mm needles and DK yarn before stuffing.

ABBREVIATIONS
See page 156

SPECIAL ABBREVIATION
s2p: slip 2 stitches pwise – slip 2 stitches pwise from LH needle to RH needle.

HOW TO MAKE WOODPECKER

BODY AND HEAD

Using the long tail method and yarn A, cast on 8 sts.

Row 1 and foll 4 alt rows: Purl.

Row 2: (Kfb) to end (16 sts).

Row 4: (Kfb, k1) to end (24 sts).

Row 6: (Kfb, k2) to end (32 sts).

Row 8: (Kfb, k3) to end (40 sts).

Row 10: (Kfb, k4) to end (48 sts).

Rows 11 to 21: Work 11 rows in st-st.

Rows 22 and 23: Work 2 rows in g-st to mark waist.

Rows 24 to 27: Beg with a k row, work 4 rows in st-st.

Row 28: Cast off 5 sts at beg of next row, k37 (38 sts now on RH needle), cast off rem 5 sts and fasten off (38 sts).

Row 29: Rejoin yarn to rem sts and p 1 row.

Row 30: K2tog, k to last 2 sts, k2tog (36 sts).

Row 31: Purl.

Rows 32 to 35: Rep rows 30 and 31 twice more (32 sts).

Rows 36 and 37: Work 2 rows in st-st.

Rows 38 to 41: Join on yarn B and work 4 rows in st-st.

Rows 42 to 45: Using yarn A, work 4 rows in st-st.

Row 46: Using yarn B, k6, s2p (see special abbreviation), k16, s2p, k6.

Row 47: P6, s2p, p16, s2p, p6.

Rows 48 and 49: Rep rows 46 and 47 once.

Rows 50 and 51: Using yarn A, work 2 rows in st-st.

Rows 52 and 53: Change to yarn C and work 2 rows in st-st.

Row 54: (K2tog, k2) to end (24 sts).

Row 55 and foll alt row: Purl.

Row 56: (K2tog, k1) to end (16 sts).

Row 58: (K2tog) to end (8 sts). Break yarn and thread through sts on needle, pull tight and secure by threading yarn a second time through sts.

DUNGAREES

Using the long tail method and yarn D, cast on 8 sts.

Row 1 and foll 5 alt rows: Purl.

Row 2: (Kfb) to end (16 sts).

Row 4: As row 2 (32 sts).

Row 6: (Kfb, k3) to end (40 sts).

Row 8: (Kfb, k4) to end (48 sts).

Row 10: (Kfb, k5) to end (56 sts).

Row 12: (Kfb, k6) to end (64 sts).

Rows 13 to 23: Beg with a p row, work 11 rows in st-st.

Rows 24 to 26: Work 3 rows in g-st, ending with a RS row.

DIVIDE FOR BIB

Row 27: Cast off 25 sts kwise, k13 (14 sts now on RH needle), cast off rem 25 sts kwise and fasten off.

Rejoin yarn to rem sts and patt:

Row 28: K2, (k1 tbl) 10 times, k2 (14 sts).

Row 29: K2, p10, k2.

Row 30: Knit.

Rows 31 to 34: Rep rows 29 and 30 twice more, ending with a k row.

Rows 35 and 36: Work 2 rows in g-st ending with a RS row. Cast off in g-st.

LEGS (make 2)

Using the long tail method and yarn E, cast on 7 sts.

Row 1: Purl.

Row 2: (Kfb) to end (14 sts).

Rows 3 to 7: Work 5 rows in st-st.

Row 8: Change to yarn D and k 1 row.

Row 9: K4, (kfb, k4) twice (16 sts).

Rows 10 to 13: Beg with a k row, work 4 rows in st-st. Cast off.

FEET AND BACK TOE, AND TOES

Work feet and back toe, and toes using yarn E, as for Owl on page 39.

TAIL (make 2 pieces)

Using the long tail method and yarn A, cast on 14 sts.

Rows 1 to 25: Beg with a p row, work 25 rows in st-st.

Row 26: (K2tog) to end (7 sts).

Break yarn and thread through sts on needle, pull tight and secure by threading yarn a second time through sts.

WINGS (make 2)

Using the long tail method and yarn A, cast on 12 sts.

Row 1 and foll 3 alt rows: Purl.

Row 2: (K1, m1, k4, m1, k1) twice (16 sts).

Row 4: (K1, m1, k6, m1, k1) twice (20 sts).

Row 6: (K1, m1, k8, m1, k1) twice (24 sts).

Row 8: (K1, m1, k10, m1, k1) twice (28 sts).

Rows 9 to 15: Work 7 rows in st-st.

Rows 16 and 17: Join on yarn B and work 2 rows in st-st.

Row 18: Yarn A-K2tog, k10, (k2tog) twice, k10, k2tog (24 sts).

Row 19: Purl.

Row 20: Yarn B-K2tog, k8, (k2tog) twice, k8, k2tog (20 sts).

Row 21: Yarn B-purl.

Row 22: Yarn A-K2tog, k6, (k2tog) twice, k6, k2tog (16 sts).

Row 23: Yarn A-purl.

Row 24: Yarn B-K2tog, k4, (k2tog) twice, k4, k2tog (12 sts).

Row 25: Yarn B-purl.

Row 26: (K2tog) to end (6 sts).

Break yarn and thread through sts on needle, pull tight and secure by threading yarn a second time through sts.

WING STRIPE (make 2)

Using the long tail method and yarn B, cast on 12 sts.

Row 1: Purl.

Cast off kwise.

STRAPS FOR DUNGAREES (make 2)

Using the long tail method and yarn D, cast on 28 sts.

Row 1: Knit.

Cast off kwise.

BEAK

Using the long tail method and yarn E, cast on 8 sts.

Rows 1 to 7: Beg with a p row, work 7 rows in st-st.

Row 8: K1, k2tog, k2, k2tog, k1 (6 sts).

Rows 9 to 11: Work 3 rows in st-st.

Break yarn and thread through sts on needle, pull tight and secure by threading yarn a second time through sts.

MAKING UP

Note: Sew up all row-end seams on right side using mattress stitch one stitch in from the edge, unless otherwise stated; a one-stitch seam allowance has been allowed for this.

BODY AND HEAD

Gather round cast-on stitches, pull tight and secure. Sew up side edges of head, down and across back to lower edge leaving a gap. Stuff head and body and sew up gap.

DUNGAREES

Sew up side edges of dungarees and place on Woodpecker. Sew top edge of dungarees to waist of body using backstitch.

LEGS

Sew up side edges of legs and stuff legs. Sew legs to underneath of Woodpecker, sewing through dungarees to body.

FEET AND TOES

Make up feet and toes, as for Owl on page 40.

TAIL

Cut two pieces of cardboard 3 x ¾in (7.5 x 2cm) and round one end. Place cardboard on wrong side of tail and fold tail lengthways enclosing cardboard inside. Sew up side edges of both halves of tail and sew tail to Woodpecker.

WINGS AND WING STRIPE

Fold wings bringing side edges together and oversew side edges and cast-on stitches. Sew a stripe to each side of wing. Sew wings to Woodpecker at each side.

STRAPS AND BUTTONS

Sew straps to each side of bib, take straps over back, cross over and sew ends of straps to top of dungarees. Add two buttons to bib.

BEAK

Fold chenille stem in half and place fold into tip of beak. Sew up side edges of beak enclosing chenille stem inside and cut excess chenille stem. Stuff beak with a tiny bit of stuffing with tweezers or tip of scissors and sew beak to head.

FEATURES

Mark position of eyes with two pins and embroider eyes in black making a chain stitch for each eye and a second chain stitch on top of first (see page 155 for how to begin and fasten off invisibly for the embroidery).

MOUSE

INFORMATION YOU'LL NEED

MATERIALS

Any DK (US: light worsted) yarn
(amounts given are approximate)
Yarn A silver grey (20g for each
mouse)
Yarn B pink (5g)
Yarn C mint (10g)
Yarn D mauve (10g)
Oddment of black for embroidery
and silver grey for making up
1 pair of 3.25mm (UK10:US3)
needles and a spare needle of same
size for dungarees
Knitters' pins and a blunt-ended
needle for sewing up
Acrylic toy stuffing
2 small buttons for each mouse

FINISHED SIZE

Mouse stands 7½in (19cm) tall

TENSION

26 sts x 34 rows measure 4in (10cm)
square over st-st using 3.25mm
needles and DK yarn before stuffing.

ABBREVIATIONS

See page 156

HOW TO MAKE MOUSE

BODY

Using the long tail method and yarn A, cast on 36 sts.

Row 1: Purl.

Row 2: K1, (k8, m1, k1, m1, k8) twice, k1 (40 sts).

Rows 3 to 7: Work 5 rows in st-st.

Rows 8 and 9: Work 2 rows in g-st to mark waist.

Rows 10 to 17: Beg with a k row, work 8 rows in st-st.

Row 18: K1, (k8, k3tog, k8) twice, k1 (36 sts).

Row 19 and foll alt row: Purl.

Row 20: K1, (k7, k3tog, k7) twice, k1 (32 sts).

Row 22: K1, (k6, k3tog, k6) twice, k1 (28 sts).

Row 23: Purl.

Cast off.

HEAD AND NOSE

Using the long tail method and yarn A, cast on 8 sts.

Row 1 and foll 3 alt rows: Purl.

Row 2: (Kfb) to end (16 sts).

Row 4: (Kfb, k1) to end (24 sts).

Row 6: (Kfb, k2) to end (32 sts).

Row 8: (Kfb, k3) to end (40 sts).

Rows 9 to 19: Work 11 rows in st-st.

Row 20: (K1, k2tog) 6 times, k4, (k2tog, k1) 6 times (28 sts).

Rows 21 to 23: Work 3 rows in st-st.

Row 24: K7, (k2tog, k2) 4 times, k5 (24 sts).

Row 25 and foll 2 alt row: Purl.

Row 26: K5, (k2tog, k2) 4 times, k3 (20 sts).

Row 28: K3, (K2tog, k2) 4 times, k1 (16 sts).

Row 30: K4, (k2tog) 4 times, k4 (12 sts).

Row 31: Purl.

Rows 32 and 33: Change to yarn B and k 1 row then p 1 row.

Row 34: (K2tog, k1) to end (8 sts). Break yarn and thread through sts on needle, pull tight and secure by threading yarn a second time through sts.

FEET AND LEGS (make 2)

Using the long tail method and yarn A, cast on 8 sts.

Row 1 and foll alt row: Purl.

Row 2: (Kfb) to end (16 sts).

Row 4: (Kfb, k1) to end (24 sts).

Rows 5 to 9: Work 5 rows in st-st.

Row 10: (K2tog, k1) to end (16 sts).

Rows 11 to 21: Work 11 rows in st-st.

Cast off.

PAWS AND FOREARMS (make 2)

Using the long tail method and yarn A, cast on 9 sts.

Row 1: Purl.

Row 2: (Kfb) to end (18 sts).

Rows 3 to 7: Work 5 rows in st-st.

Row 8: (K2tog, k1) to end (12 sts).

Rows 9 to 21: Work 13 rows in st-st.

Row 22: (K2tog, k1) to end (8 sts). Break yarn, thread through sts on needle and leave loose.

DUNGAREES
(make 2 pieces)
Note: foll individual instructions as given for 1 front and 1 back of dungarees.

FIRST LEG
Using the long tail method and yarn C, cast on 12 sts and beg in g-st.

Rows 1 and 2: Work 2 rows in g-st.
Break yarn and set aside.

SECOND LEG
Work as for first leg but do not break yarn.

JOIN LEGS
Row 3: Beg with second leg and k10, k2tog, turn, using the knitting-on method, cast on 5 sts, turn, then with the same yarn continue across first leg and k2tog, k to end (27 sts).

Row 4 and foll 2 alt rows: Purl.

Row 5: K2, m1, k23, m1, k2 (29 sts).

Row 7: K12, k2tog, k1, k2tog, k12 (27 sts).

Row 9: K10, k2tog, k3, k2tog, k10 (25 sts).

Rows 10 to 12: Work 3 rows in st-st.

Rows 13 to 15: Work 3 rows in g-st, ending with a RS row.
Cast off in g-st for back of dungarees or cont with bib for front of dungarees:

DIVIDE FOR BIB
Row 16: Cast off 7 sts kwise, k10 (11 sts now on RH needle), cast off rem 7 sts and fasten off.
Rejoin yarn to rem sts and patt:

**Row 17: K2, (k1 tbl) 7 times, k2 (11 sts).

Row 18: K2, p7, k2.

Row 19: Knit.

Rows 20 to 25: Rep rows 18 and 19, 3 times more, ending with a k row.

Rows 26 and 27: Work 2 rows in g-st, ending with a RS row.
Cast off in g-st.

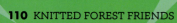

STRAPS FOR DUNGAREES
(make 2)
Using the long tail method and yarn C, cast on 25 sts.
Row 1: Knit.
Cast off kwise.

PINAFORE
Using the long tail method and yarn D, cast on 65 sts and beg in g-st.
Rows 1 and 2: Work 2 rows in g-st.
Rows 3 to 12: Beg with a k row, work 10 rows in st-st.
Row 13: K1, (k2tog, k2) to end (49 sts).
Rows 14 and 15: Work 2 rows in g-st, ending with a RS row.
DIVIDE FOR BIB
Row 16: Cast off 19 sts kwise, k10 (11 sts now on RH needle), cast off rem 19 sts and fasten off. Rejoin yarn to rem sts and work bib from **, as for dungarees.

STRAPS FOR PINAFORE
(make 2)
Make straps for pinafore using yarn D, as for dungarees.

EARS (make 2)
Using the long tail method and yarn A, cast on 13 sts.
Row 1: Purl.
Row 2: (Kfb) to end (26 sts).
Rows 3 to 11: Beg with a p row, work 9 rows in st-st.
Row 12: K2tog, (k1, k2tog) to end (17 sts).
Row 13: Purl.
Row 14: K2tog, (k1, k2tog) to end (11 sts).
Row 15: Purl.
Break yarn and thread through sts on needle, pull tight and secure by threading yarn a second time through sts.

MAKING UP

Note: Sew up all row-end seams on right side using mattress stitch one stitch in from the edge, unless otherwise stated; a one-stitch seam allowance has been allowed for this.

BODY AND TAIL

Make a twisted cord for tail using four strands of yarn beginning with each 36in (91cm) long (see page 155). Tie a tight knot 7in (18cm) from folded end and trim ends. Sew up side edges of body and enclose knot of tail in seam just below waist, securing on wrong side. With this seam at centre back, oversew cast-on stitches. Stuff body leaving neck open.

HEAD AND NOSE

Gather round cast-on stitches of head and sew up side edges of head leaving a gap, stuff head and sew up gap. Pin and sew head to body.

FEET AND LEGS

Gather round cast-on stitches of feet, pull tight and secure. Stuff feet and sew up side edges of legs and stuff legs. Pin legs to body leaving a ¾in (2cm) gap at crotch and sew in place.

PAWS AND FOREARMS

Gather round cast-on stitches of paws, pull tight and secure. Stuff paws and sew up side edges of arms and stuff arms. Pull stitches on a thread tight and secure, and sew arms to Mouse at each side.

DUNGAREES OR PINAFORE, STRAPS AND BUTTONS

Place two pieces of dungarees together matching all edges and sew up inside leg seams and across crotch, and sew up side seams. Or, sew up side edges of skirt of pinafore. Place tip of tail through dungarees or pinafore below waist band at back. Place dungarees or pinafore on Mouse.

Sew cast-off stitches of waist of dungarees or pinafore to row above waist of Mouse using backstitch all the way round. Sew ends of straps to top edge of front of bib at each side, take straps over shoulders, cross over and sew to back of dungarees or pinafore. Add two buttons to bib.

EARS

Sew up side edges of ears and with seam at centre back, press flat. Position ears and pin and sew ears to head.

FEATURES

Mark position of eyes with two pins and embroider eyes in black making a vertical chain stitch for each eye, then a second chain stitch on top of first. Embroider eyebrows in black using straight stitches (see page 155 for how to begin and fasten off invisibly for the embroidery).

FROG

INFORMATION YOU'LL NEED

MATERIALS
Any DK (US: light worsted) yarn
(amounts given are approximate)
Yarn A green (20g for each frog)
Yarn B white (5g)
Yarn C petrol blue (10g)
Yarn D purple (10g)
Oddment of black for embroidery
1 pair of 3.25mm (UK10:US3) needles
and a spare needle of same size for
dungarees
Knitters' pins and a blunt-ended needle
for sewing up
Tweezers (optional)
Acrylic toy stuffing
2 small buttons for each frog
12 chenille stems for each frog

FINISHED SIZE
Frog stands 7½in (19cm) tall

TENSION
26 sts x 34 rows measure 4in (10cm)
square over st-st using 3.25mm needles
and DK yarn before stuffing.

ABBREVIATIONS
See page 156

HOW TO MAKE FROG

BODY

Using the long tail method and yarn A, cast on 28 sts.

Row 1: Purl.

Row 2: K1, (k6, m1, k1, m1, k6) twice, k1 (32 sts).

Rows 3 to 11: Work 9 rows in st-st.

Rows 12 and 13: Work 2 rows in g-st to mark waist.

Rows 14 to 25: Beg with a k row, work 12 rows in st-st.

Row 26: (K2tog, k2) to end (24 sts).

Row 27: Purl.

Cast off.

HEAD

Using the long tail method and yarn A, cast on 24 sts.

Row 1: Purl.

Row 2: (Kfb, k2) to end (32 sts).

Rows 3 to 17: Beg with a p row. work 15 rows in st-st.

Row 18: (K2tog, k2) to end (24 sts).

Row 19 and foll alt row: Purl.

Row 20: (K2tog, k1) to end (16 sts).

Row 22: (K2tog) to end (8 sts).

Break yarn and thread through sts on needle, pull tight and secure by threading yarn a second time through sts.

MOUTH

Using the long tail method and yarn A, cast on 32 sts.

Rows 1 and 2: P 1 row then k 1 row.

Row 3: P4, (p2tog) 4 times, p8, (p2tog) 4 times, p4 (24 sts).

Row 4: Knit.

Row 5: P2, (p2tog) 4 times, p4, (p2tog) 4 times, p2 (16 sts).

Cast off.

EYES (make 2)

Using the long tail method and yarn A, cast on 7 sts.

Row 1: Purl.

Row 2: K1, (m1, k1) to end (13 sts).

Rows 3 to 6: Work 4 rows in st-st, ending with RS row.

Row 7: Knit.

Rows 8 and 9: Change to yarn B and k 1 row then p 1 row.

Row 10: K1, (k2tog, k1) to end (9 sts).

Break yarn and thread through sts on needle, pull tight and secure by threading yarn a second time through sts.

LEGS (make 2)

Using the long tail method and yarn A, cast on 14 sts.

Row 1 to 13: Beg with a p row, work 13 rows in st-st.

Row 14: K2tog, (k1, k2tog) to end (9 sts).

Rows 15 to 23: Work 9 rows in st-st.

Break yarn and thread through sts on needle, pull tight and secure by threading yarn a second time through sts.

FOREARMS (make 2)

Using the long tail method and yarn A, cast on 11 sts.

Rows 1 to 11: Beg with a p row, work 11 rows in st-st.

Row 12: K2tog, k7, k2tog (9 sts).

Rows 13 to 19: Work 7 rows in st-st.

Break yarn and thread through sts on needle, pull tight and secure by threading yarn a second time through sts.

DUNGAREES
(make 2 pieces)

Note: foll individual instructions as given for 1 front and 1 back of dungarees.

FIRST LEG

Using the long tail method and yarn C, cast on 11 sts and beg in g-st.

Rows 1 and 2: Work 2 rows in g-st.

Break yarn and set aside.

SECOND LEG

Work as for first leg but do not break yarn.

JOIN LEGS

Row 3: Beg with second leg and k9, k2tog, turn, using the knitting-on method cast on 5 sts, turn, then with the same yarn continue across first leg and k2tog, k to end (25 sts).

Rows 4 to 6: Beg with a p row, work 3 rows in st-st.

Row 7: K10, k2tog, k1, k2tog, k10 (23 sts).

Row 8: Purl.

Row 9: K8, k2tog, k3, k2tog, k8 (21 sts).

Rows 10 to 16: Work 7 rows in st-st.

Rows 17 to 19: Work 3 rows in g-st, ending with a RS row.

Cast off in g-st for back of dungarees or cont with bib for front of dungarees:

DIVIDE FOR BIB

Row 20: Cast off 6 sts kwise, k8 (9 sts now on RH needle), cast off rem 6 sts and fasten off.

Rejoin yarn to rem sts and patt:

Row 21: K2, (k1 tbl) 5 times, k2 (9 sts).

Row 22: K2, p5, k2.

Row 23: Knit.

Rows 24 to 27: Rep rows 22 and 23, twice more, ending with a k row.

Rows 28 and 29: Work 2 rows in g-st, ending with a RS row. Cast off in g-st.

STRAPS FOR DUNGAREES (make 2)

Using the long tail method and yarn C, cast on 26 sts.

Row 1: Knit.

Cast off kwise.

PINAFORE

Using the long tail method and yarn D, cast on 54 sts and beg in g-st.

Rows 1 and 2: Work 2 rows in g-st.

Rows 3 to 16: Beg with a k row, work 14 rows in st-st.

Row 17: K2, (k2tog, k2) to end (41 sts).

Rows 18 and 19: Work 2 rows in g-st, ending with a RS row.

DIVIDE FOR BIB

Row 20: Cast off 16 sts kwise, k8 (9 sts now on RH needle), cast off rem 16 sts and fasten off.

Rejoin yarn to rem sts and work bib from **, as for dungarees.

STRAPS FOR PINAFORE

Make straps using yarn D, as for dungarees.

TOES (make 6)

Using the long tail method and yarn A, cast on 6 sts.

Rows 1 to 5: Beg with a p row, work 5 rows in st-st.

Row 6: K1, (m1, k1) to end (11 sts).

Rows 7 to 9: Work 3 rows in st-st. Break yarn and thread through sts on needle, pull tight and secure by threading yarn a second time through sts.

FINGERS (make 6)

Using the long tail method and yarn A, cast on 6 sts.

Rows 1 to 3: Beg with a p row, work 3 rows in st-st.

Row 4: K1, (m1, k1) to end (11 sts).

Rows 5 to 7: Work 3 rows in st-st. Break yarn and thread through sts on needle, pull tight and secure by threading yarn a second time through sts.

MAKING UP

Note: Sew up all row-end seams on right side using mattress stitch one stitch in from the edge, unless otherwise stated; a one-stitch seam allowance has been allowed for this.

BODY

Sew up side edges of body and with this seam at centre back, oversew cast-on stitches. Stuff body leaving neck open.

HEAD AND MOUTH

Sew up side edges of head and stuff head. Pin head to body and sew head to body making a horizontal stitch from head, then a horizontal stitch from body and do this alternately all the way round. Sew up side edges of mouth and with this seam at centre of underneath, sew across cast-on stitches. Stuff mouth, pin to front of head low down and sew in place.

EYES

Gather round cast-on stitches of eyes, pull tight and secure. Sew up side edges of eyes leaving a gap, stuff with tweezers or tip of scissors and sew up gap. Sew eyes to sides of head.

LEGS AND FOREARMS

Take three chenille stems and fold in half. Place fold on stitches pulled tight on a thread on wrong side of leg and sew up side edges of leg enclosing chenille stems inside. Repeat for other leg and forearms and place a little stuffing inside the wide part with tweezers or tip of scissors. Cut excess chenille stems. Gather round cast-on stitches of arms, pull tight and secure. Pin legs to body leaving a ¾in (2cm) gap at crotch, sew in place and bend legs. Sew top of arms to below neck and bend arms.

DUNGAREES, STRAPS AND BUTTONS

Make up dungarees, straps and buttons, as for Deer on page 22.

PINAFORE, STRAPS AND BUTTONS

Make up pinafore, straps and buttons, as for Deer on page 22.

TOES AND FINGERS

Sew up side edges of each toe and finger. Sew three fingers and toes together at base of each finger and toe and sew to ends of each arm and leg.

FEATURES

Embroider eyes in black making a long vertical chain stitch for each eye, then a second chain stitch on top of first. Embroider mouth using stem stitch (see page 155 for how to begin and fasten off invisibly for the embroidery).

WOLF

INFORMATION YOU'LL NEED

MATERIALS

Any DK (US: light worsted) yarn
(amounts given are approximate)
Yarn A dark grey (25g)
Yarn B cream (10g)
Yarn C black (5g)
Yarn D claret (10g)
Yarn E slate grey (10g)
Oddment of black for embroidery
1 pair of 3.25mm (UK10:US3)
needles and a spare needle
of same size
2 yarn bobbins
Knitters' pins and a blunt-ended
needle for sewing up
Acrylic toy stuffing
2 small buttons

FINISHED SIZE

Wolf stands 7½in (19cm) tall

TENSION

26 sts x 34 rows measure 4in (10cm)
square over st-st using 3.25mm
needles and DK yarn before stuffing.

ABBREVIATIONS

See page 156

HOW TO MAKE WOLF

BODY

Note: before beg, wind a bobbin in yarn A and reserve.
Using the long tail method and yarn A, cast on 36 sts.
Row 1: Purl.
Row 2: K1, (k8, m1, k1, m1, k8) twice, k1 (40 sts).
Rows 3 to 7: Work 5 rows in st-st.
Rows 8 and 9: Work 2 rows in g-st to mark waist.
Rows 10 to 15: Beg with a k row, work 6 rows in st-st.
Join on yarn B and bobbin of yarn A and work in intarsia twisting yarn when changing colours to avoid a hole.
Row 16: Yarn A-k19, yarn B-k2, yarn A (bobbin)-k19.
Row 17: Yarn A-p18, yarn B-p4, yarn A-p18.
Row 18: Yarn A-k9, k3tog, k5, yarn B-k6, yarn A-k5, k3tog, k9 (36 sts).
Row 19: Yarn A-p15, yarn B-p6, yarn A-p15.
Row 20: Yarn A-k8, k3tog, k3, yarn B-k8, yarn A-k3, k3tog, k8 (32 sts).
Row 21: Yarn A-p12, yarn B-p8, yarn A-p12.
Row 22: Yarn A-k7, k3tog, k1, yarn B-k10, yarn A-k1, k3tog, k7 (28 sts).
Row 23: Yarn A-p9, yarn B-p10, yarn A-p9.

Row 24: Yarn A-k6, k3tog, yarn B-k10, yarn A-k3tog, k6 (24 sts).
Row 25: Yarn A-p7, yarn B-p10, yarn A-p7.
Cast off in colours as set.

HEAD

Note: before beg wind a yarn bobbin in yarn B and reserve.
Using the long tail method and yarn A, cast on 8 sts.
Row 1 and foll 3 alt rows: Purl.
Row 2: (Kfb) to end (16 sts).
Row 4: (Kfb, k1) to end (24 sts).
Row 6: (Kfb, k2) to end (32 sts).
Row 8: (Kfb, k3) to end (40 sts).
Rows 9 to 17: Work 9 rows in st-st.
Row 18: K1, (k2tog, k2) to last 3 sts, k2tog, k1 (30 sts).
Rows 19 to 21: Work 3 rows in st-st.
Join on yarn B and bobbin of yarn B and rejoin yarn A and work in intarsia, twisting yarn when changing colours to avoid a hole:
Row 22: Yarn B-k8, k2tog, k1, yarn A-k8, Yarn B-k1, k2tog, k8 (28 sts).
Row 23: Yarn B-p10, yarn A-p8, yarn B-p10.
Row 24: Yarn B-k7, k2tog, k1, yarn A-k1, k2tog, k2, k2tog, k1, yarn B-k1, k2tog, k7 (24 sts).
Row 25: Yarn B-p9, yarn A-p6, yarn B-p9.

Row 26: Yarn B-(k2tog, k1) 3 times, yarn A-k6, yarn B-(k1, k2tog) 3 times (18 sts).
Row 27: Yarn B-p6, yarn A-p6, yarn B-p6.
Row 28: Yarn B-k6, yarn A-k1, (k2tog) twice, k1, yarn B-k6 (16 sts).
Row 29: Yarn B-p6, yarn A-p4, yarn B-p6.
Change to yarn C and dec:
Row 30: (K2tog) to end (8 sts).
Rows 31 to 33: Work 3 rows in st-st.
Break yarn and thread through sts on needle, pull tight and secure by threading yarn a second time through sts.

FEET AND LEGS (make 2)

Using the long tail method and yarn A, cast on 16 sts.
Row 1: Purl.
Row 2: (K1, kfb) 4 times, (kfb, k1) 4 times (24 sts).
Rows 3 to 7: Work 5 rows in st-st.
Row 8: K6, (k2tog) 6 times, k6 (18 sts).
Row 9: Purl.
Row 10: K7, (k2tog) twice, k7 (16 sts).
Rows 11 to 21: Work 11 rows in st-st.
Cast off.

PAWS AND FOREARMS (make 2)

Using the long tail method and yarn A, cast on 10 sts.
Row 1: Purl.
Row 2: (Kfb) to end (20 sts).
Rows 3 to 5: Work 3 rows in st-st.
Row 6: (K2tog, k2) to end (15 sts).
Rows 7 to 21: Work 15 rows in st-st.
Row 22: (K2tog, k1) to end (10 sts).
Break yarn, thread through sts on needle and leave loose.

TROUSERS (make 2 pieces)

FIRST LEG

Using the long tail method and yarn D, cast on 12 sts and beg in g-st.
Rows 1 and 2: Work 2 rows in g-st.
Break yarn and set aside.

SECOND LEG

Work as for first leg but do not break yarn.

JOIN LEGS

Row 3: Beg with second leg and k10, k2tog, turn, using the knitting-on method cast on 5 sts, turn, then with the same yarn continue across first leg and k2tog, k to end (27 sts).
Row 4 and foll 2 alt rows: Purl.
Row 5: K2, m1, k23, m1, k2 (29 sts).
Row 7: K12, k2tog, k1, k2tog, k12 (27 sts).

Row 9: K10, k2tog, k3, k2tog, k10 (25 sts).
Rows 10 to 12: Work 3 rows in st-st.
Rows 13 to 15: Work 3 rows in g-st, ending with a RS row.
Cast off in g-st.

BRACES (make 2)

Using the long tail method and yarn E, cast on 30 sts.
Row 1: Knit.
Cast off kwise.

EARS (make 2)

OUTER EAR

Using the long tail method and yarn A, cast on 11 sts.
Rows 1 to 3: Beg with a p row, work 3 rows in st-st.
Row 4: K2, k2tog, k3, k2tog, k2 (9 sts).
Row 5 and foll alt row: Purl.
Row 6: K3, k3tog, k3 (7 sts).
Row 8: K2, k3tog, k2 (5 sts).
Break yarn and thread through sts on needle, pull tight and secure by threading yarn a second time through sts.

INSIDE EAR

Using the long tail method and yarn B, cast on 6 sts.
Rows 1 to 3: Beg with a p row, work 3 rows in st-st.
Row 4: K1, (k2tog) twice, k1 (4 sts).
Row 5: Purl.
Break yarn and thread through

sts on needle, pull tight and secure by threading yarn a second time through sts.

TAIL

Using the long tail method and yarn A, cast on 10 sts.
Rows 1 to 5: Beg with a p row, work 5 rows in st-st.
Row 6: K3, m1, k4, m1, k3 (12 sts).
Rows 7 to 11: Work 5 rows in st-st.
Row 12: K4, m1, k4, m1, k4 (14 sts).
Rows 13 to 17: Work 5 rows in st-st.
Row 18: K4, m1, k6, m1, k4 (16 sts).
Rows 19 to 23: Work 5 rows in st-st.
Rows 24 to 27: Change to yarn B and work 4 rows in g-st.
Row 28: (K2tog, k2) to end (12 sts).
Rows 29 to 31: Work 3 rows in st-st.
Row 32: (K2tog, k1) to end (8 sts).
Row 33: Purl.
Row 34: (K2tog) to end (4 sts).
Break yarn and thread through sts on needle, pull tight and secure by threading yarn a second time through sts.

MAKING UP

Note: Sew up all row-end seams on right side using mattress stitch one stitch in from the edge, unless otherwise stated; a one-stitch seam allowance has been allowed for this.

BODY

Sew up side edges of body and with this seam at centre back, oversew cast-on stitches. Stuff body leaving neck open.

HEAD

Weave in ends around intarsia. Gather round cast-on stitches of head, pull tight and secure. Sew up side edges leaving a gap, stuff head, pushing stuffing into nose and sew up gap. Pin and sew head to body with nose pointing down.

FEET AND LEGS

Fold cast-on stitches of feet in half and oversew. Sew up side edges of feet and legs and stuff. Pin legs to body leaving a ¾in (2cm) gap at crotch and sew in place.

PAWS AND FOREARMS

Gather round cast-on stitches of paws, pull tight and secure. Sew up side edges of paws and forearms and stuff. Pull stitches on a thread tight and secure. Sew forearms to body of Wolf at each side.

TROUSERS, BRACES AND BUTTONS

Place two pieces of trousers together matching all edges, sew up inside leg seams and across crotch. Sew up side seams and place trousers on Wolf. Sew trousers to row above waist of Wolf using backstitch. Sew ends of braces to front of trousers, take braces over shoulders, cross over and sew to back waist. Add two buttons to front of trousers.

EARS

Sew up side edges of last three rows of outer ears and place inner ear inside outer ear with wrong sides together. Sew side edges together. Position ears and pin and sew ears to head.

FEATURES

Mark position of eyes with two pins and embroider eyes in black making a vertical chain stitch for each eye, then a second chain stitch on top of first. Embroider eyebrows in black using long stitches (see page 155 for how to begin and fasten off invisibly for the embroidery).

TAIL

Sew up side edges of wide part of tail and stuff. Finish sewing up side edges adding a little stuffing. Sew tail to back below waistband, sewing through trousers to body.

KIWI

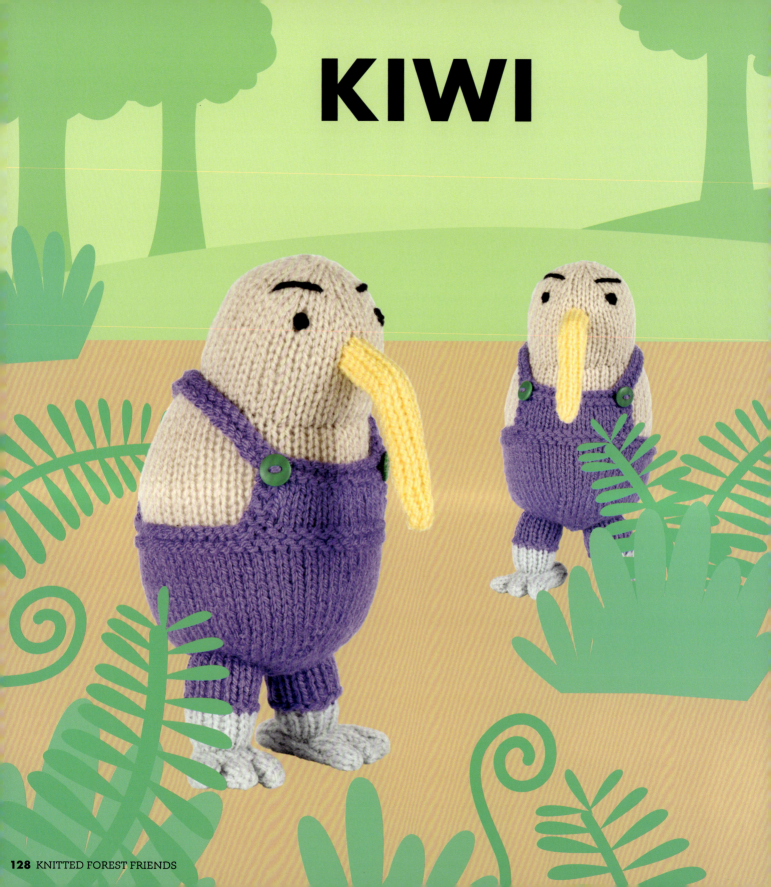

INFORMATION YOU'LL NEED

MATERIALS
Any DK (US: light worsted) yarn
(amounts given are approximate)
Yarn A beige (20g)
Yarn B lavender (10g)
Yarn C silver grey (5g)
Yarn D lemon (5g)
Oddment of black for embroidery
1 pair of 3.25mm (UK10:US3)
needles
Knitters' pins and a blunt-ended
needle for sewing up
Tweezers (optional)
Acrylic toy stuffing
2 chenille stems
2 small buttons

FINISHED SIZE
Kiwi stands 7½in (19cm) tall

TENSION
26 sts x 34 rows measure 4in (10cm)
square over st-st using 3.25mm
needles and DK yarn before stuffing.

ABBREVIATIONS
See page 156

HOW TO MAKE KIWI

BODY
Using the long tail method and yarn A, cast on 8 sts.

Row 1 and foll 4 alt rows: Purl.
Row 2: (Kfb) to end (16 sts).
Row 4: (Kfb, k1) to end (24 sts).
Row 6: (Kfb, k2) to end (32 sts).
Row 8: (Kfb, k3) to end (40 sts).
Row 10: (Kfb, k4) to end (48 sts).
Rows 11 to 23: Work 13 rows in st-st.
Rows 24 and 25: Work 2 rows in g-st for waist.
Rows 26 to 43: Beg with a k row, work 18 rows in st-st.
Row 44: (K2tog, k4) to end (40 sts).
Row 45 and foll 3 alt rows: Purl.
Row 46: (K2tog, k3) to end (32 sts).
Row 48: (K2tog, k2) to end (24 sts).
Row 50: (K2tog, k1) to end (16 sts).
Row 52: (K2tog) to end (8 sts).
Break yarn and thread through sts on needle, pull tight and secure by threading yarn a second time through sts.

HEAD
Using the long tail method and yarn A, cast on 40 sts.
Rows 1 to 13: Beg with a p row, work 13 rows in st-st.

Row 14: (K2tog, k3) to end (32 sts).
Row 15 and foll 2 alt rows: Purl.
Row 16: (K2tog, k2) to end (24 sts).
Row 18: (K2tog, k1) to end (16 sts).
Row 20: (K2tog) to end (8 sts).
Break yarn and thread through sts on needle, pull tight and secure by threading yarn a second time through sts.

DUNGAREES
(make 2 pieces)
Using the long tail method and yarn B, cast on 12 sts.
Row 1 and foll 5 alt rows: Purl.
Row 2: (Kfb) to end (24 sts).
Row 4: (Kfb, k2) to end (32 sts).
Row 6: (Kfb, k3) to end (40 sts).
Row 8: (Kfb, k4) to end (48 sts).
Row 10: (Kfb, k5) to end (56 sts).
Row 12: (Kfb, k6) to end (64 sts).
Rows 13 to 23: Work 11 rows in st-st.
Rows 24 to 26: Work 3 rows in g-st.

DIVIDE FOR BIB
Row 27: Cast off 24 sts kwise, k15 (16 sts now an RH needle), cast off rem 24 sts kwise and fasten off.
Rejoin yarn to rem sts and patt:
Row 28: K2, (k1 tbl) 12 times, k2 (16 sts).

Row 29: K2, p12, k2.
Row 30: Knit.
Rows 31 to 34: Rep rows 29 and 30 twice more, ending with a k row.
Rows 35 and 36: Work 2 rows in g-st, ending with a RS row.
Cast off in g-st.

STRAPS FOR DUNGAREES
(make 2)
Using the long tail method and yarn B, cast on 40 sts.
Row 1: Knit.
Cast off kwise.

LEGS (make 2)
Using the long tail method and yarn C, cast on 7 sts.
Row 1: Purl.
Row 2: (Kfb) to end (14 sts).
Rows 3 to 7: Work 5 rows in st-st.
Row 8: Change to yarn B and k 1 row.
Row 9: K4, (kfb, k4) twice (16 sts).
Row 10 to 15: Beg with a k row, work 6 rows in st-st.
Cast off.

FEET AND BACK TOE
(make 2)
Work feet and back toe using yarn C, as for Owl on page 39.

BEAK

Using the long tail method and yarn D, cast on 10 sts.

Rows 1 to 9: Beg with a p row, work 9 rows in st-st.

Row 10: K2, (k2tog, k2) twice (8 sts).

Rows 11 to 21: Work 11 rows in st-st.

Row 22: K1, k2tog, k2, k2tog, k1 (6 sts).

Rows 23 to 25: Work 3 rows in st-st.

Break yarn and thread through sts on needle, pull tight and secure by threading yarn a second time through sts.

MAKING UP

Note: Sew up all row-end seams on right side using mattress stitch one stitch in from the edge, unless otherwise stated; a one-stitch seam allowance has been allowed for this.

BODY

Gather round cast-on stitches, pull tight and secure. Sew up side edges of body leaving a gap, stuff body and sew up gap.

HEAD

Sew up row ends of head and stuff head. Pin and sew head to body in a forward position.

DUNGAREES, STRAPS AND BUTTONS

Sew up side edges of dungarees and place on Kiwi. Sew top edge of dungarees to waist of body using backstitch. Sew straps to each side of bib, take straps over back, cross over and sew ends of straps to top of dungarees. Also sew middle of straps to body. Add two buttons to bib.

LEGS

Sew up side edges of legs and stuff. Sew legs to underneath of Kiwi. sewing through dungarees to body.

FEET AND TOES

Make up feet and toes, as for Owl on page 40.

BEAK

Take two chenille stems together and fold in half. Place fold of chenille stems into stitches pulled tight on a thread on wrong side of beak and sew up row ends of beak enclosing chenille stems inside. Cut excess chenille stems, sew beak to head and bend beak.

FEATURES

Mark position of eyes with two pins and embroider eyes in black making a vertical chain stitch for each eye and a second chain stitch on top of first. Embroider eyebrows in black using straight stitches (see page 155 for how to begin and fasten off invisibly for the embroidery).

OTTER

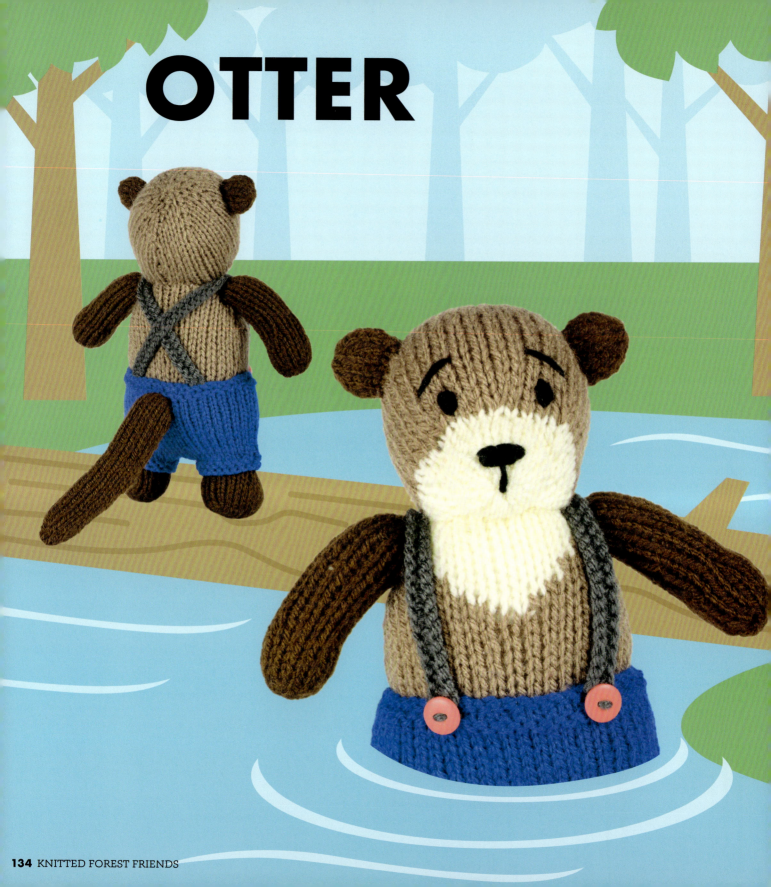

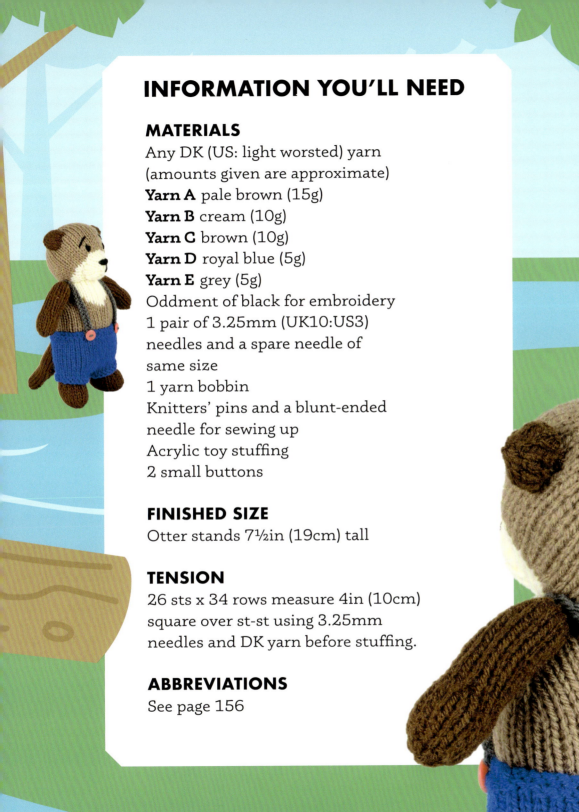

INFORMATION YOU'LL NEED

MATERIALS

Any DK (US: light worsted) yarn
(amounts given are approximate)
Yarn A pale brown (15g)
Yarn B cream (10g)
Yarn C brown (10g)
Yarn D royal blue (5g)
Yarn E grey (5g)
Oddment of black for embroidery
1 pair of 3.25mm (UK10:US3)
needles and a spare needle of
same size
1 yarn bobbin
Knitters' pins and a blunt-ended
needle for sewing up
Acrylic toy stuffing
2 small buttons

FINISHED SIZE

Otter stands 7½in (19cm) tall

TENSION

26 sts x 34 rows measure 4in (10cm)
square over st-st using 3.25mm
needles and DK yarn before stuffing.

ABBREVIATIONS

See page 156

HOW TO MAKE OTTER

BODY

Note: before beg, wind a bobbin in yarn A and reserve.

Using the long tail method and yarn A, cast on 36 sts.

Row 1: Purl.

Row 2: K1, (k8, m1, k1, m1, k8) twice, k1 (40 sts).

Rows 3 to 13: Work 11 rows in st-st.

Rows 14 and 15: Work 2 rows in g-st to mark waist.

Rows 16 to 23: Beg with a k row, work 8 rows in st-st.

Join on yarn B and bobbin of yarn A and work in intarsia in blocks of colour twisting yarn when changing colours to avoid a hole.

Row 24: Yarn A-k19, yarn B-k2, yarn A (bobbin)-k19.

Row 25: Yarn A-p18, yarn B-p4, yarn A-p18.

Row 26: Yarn A-k9, k3tog, k5, yarn B-k6, yarn A-k5, k3tog, k9 (36 sts).

Row 27: Yarn A-p15, yarn B-p6, yarn A-p15.

Row 28: Yarn A-k8, k3tog, k3, yarn B-k8, yarn A-k3, k3tog, k8 (32 sts).

Row 29: Yarn A-p12, yarn B-p8, yarn A-p12.

Row 30: Yarn A-k7, k3tog, k1, yarn B-k10, yarn A-k1, k3tog, k7 (28 sts).

Row 31: Yarn A-p9, yarn B-p10, yarn A-p9.

Row 32: Yarn A-k6, k3tog, yarn B-k10, yarn A-k3tog, k6 (24 sts).

Row 33: Yarn A-p7, yarn B-p10, yarn A-p7.

Row 34: Yarn A-k7, yarn B-k10, yarn A-k7.

Cast off in colours as set.

HEAD

Using the long tail method and yarn A, cast on 8 sts.

Row 1 and foll 3 alt rows: Purl.

Row 2: (Kfb) to end (16 sts).

Row 4: (Kfb, k1) to end (24 sts).

Row 6: (Kfb, k2) to end (32 sts).

Row 8: (Kfb, k3) to end (40 sts).

Rows 9 to 21: Work 13 rows in st-st.

Change to yarn B and dec:

Row 22: (K2tog, k3) to end (32 sts).

Row 23 and foll 2 alt rows: Purl.

Row 24: (K2tog, k2) to end (24 sts).

Row 26: (K2tog, k1) to end (16 sts).

Row 28: (K2tog) to end (8 sts).

Break yarn and thread through sts on needle, pull tight and secure by threading yarn a second time through sts.

SNOUT

Using the long tail method and yarn B, cast on 18 sts.

Rows 1 to 3: Beg with a p row, work 3 rows in st-st.

Row 4: (K2tog, k1) to end (12 sts).

Row 5: Purl.

Row 6: (K2tog) to end (6 sts).

Break yarn and thread through sts on needle, pull tight and secure by threading yarn a second time through sts.

FEET AND LEGS (make 2)

Using the long tail method and yarn C, cast on 16 sts.

Row 1: Purl.

Row 2: (K1, kfb) 4 times, (kfb, k1) 4 times (24 sts).

Rows 3 to 7: Work 5 rows in st-st.

Row 8: K4, (k2tog) 8 times, k4 (16 sts).

Rows 9 to 13: Work 5 rows in st-st.

Cast off.

PAWS AND FOREARMS (make 2)

Using the long tail method and yarn C, cast on 8 sts.

Row 1: Purl.

Row 2: (Kfb) to end (16 sts).

Rows 3 to 7: Work 5 rows in st-st.

Row 8: (K2tog, k2) to end (12 sts).

Rows 9 to 21: Work 13 rows in st-st.

Row 22: (K2tog, k1) to end (8 sts).

Break yarn, thread through sts on needle and leave loose.

TROUSERS (make 2 pieces)

FIRST LEG

Using the long tail method and yarn D, cast on 12 sts and beg in g-st.

Rows 1 and 2: Work 2 rows in g-st.

Break yarn and set aside.

SECOND LEG

Work as for first leg but do not break yarn.

JOIN LEGS

Row 3: Beg with second leg and k10, k2tog, turn, using the knitting-on method cast on 5 sts, turn, then with the same yarn continue across first leg and k2tog, k to end (27 sts).

Row 4 and foll 2 alt rows: Purl.

Row 5: K2, m1, k23, m1, k2 (29 sts).

Row 7: K12, k2tog, k1, k2tog, k12 (27 sts).

Row 9: K10, k2tog, k3, k2tog, k10 (25 sts).

Rows 10 to 18: Work 9 rows in st-st.

Rows 19 to 21: Work 3 rows in g-st, ending with a RS row.

Cast off in g-st.

BRACES (make 2)

Using the long tail method and yarn E, cast on 36 sts.

Row 1: Knit.

Cast off kwise.

EARS (make 2)

Using the long tail method and yarn C, cast on 8 sts.

Row 1: Purl.

Row 2: K1, (m1, k1) to end (15 sts).

Rows 3 to 5: Work 3 rows in st-st.

Row 6: (K2tog, k1) to end (10 sts).

Break yarn and thread through sts on needle, pull tight and secure by threading yarn a second time through sts.

TAIL

Using the long tail method and yarn C, cast on 30 sts.

Rows 1 to 3: Beg with a p row, work 3 rows in st-st.

Row 4: K2tog, k to end (29 sts).

Row 5: Purl.

Rows 6 to 33: Rep rows 4 and 5, 14 times more (15 sts).

Row 34: (K2tog, k1) to end (10 sts).

Row 35: Purl.

Break yarn and thread through sts on needle, pull tight and secure by threading yarn a second time through sts.

MAKING UP

Note: Sew up all row-end seams on right side using mattress stitch one stitch in from the edge, unless otherwise stated; a one-stitch seam allowance has been allowed for this.

BODY

Weave in ends around intarsia. Sew up side edges of body and with this seam at centre back, oversew cast-on stitches. Stuff body leaving neck open.

HEAD

Gather round cast-on stitches of head, pull tight and secure. Sew up side edges leaving a gap, stuff head and sew up gap. Pin and sew head to body matching up cream with neck of body.

FEET AND LEGS

Fold cast-on stitches of feet in half and oversew. Sew up side edges of feet and legs and stuff. Pin legs to body, with toes pointing outwards, leaving a ¾in (2cm) gap at crotch and sew in place.

PAWS AND FOREARMS

Gather round cast-on stitches of paws, pull tight and secure. Sew up side edges of paws and place a small ball of stuffing into paws. Sew up side edges of arms, stuff, and pull stitches on a thread tight and secure. Sew forearms to body of Otter at each side.

TROUSERS, BRACES AND BUTTONS

Place two pieces of trousers together matching all edges, sew up inside leg seams and across crotch. Sew up side seams and place trousers on Otter. Sew trousers to row above waist of Otter using backstitch. Sew ends of straps to front of trousers, take straps over shoulders, cross over and sew to back waist, and sew straps in place. Add two buttons to front of trousers.

EARS

Sew up side edges of ears and with seam at centre back, press flat. Position ears and pin and sew ears to head.

FEATURES

Mark position of eyes with two pins and embroider eyes in black making a vertical chain stitch for each eye, then a second chain stitch on top of first. Embroider eyebrows in black using long stitches. Embroider nose using satin stitch and a straight stitch (see page 155 for how to begin and fasten off invisibly for the embroidery).

TAIL

Roll tail up from decreasing row ends to long edge and sew long edge down. Gather round cast-on stitches, pull tight and secure. Sew tail to back below waistband, sewing through trousers to body.

ORANGUTAN

INFORMATION YOU'LL NEED

MATERIALS

Any DK (US: light worsted) yarn
(amounts given are approximate)
Yarn A burnt orange (20g)
Yarn B golden cream (5g)
Yarn C pale brown (10g)
Yarn D sapphire blue (10g)
Oddment of black for embroidery
1 pair of 3.25mm (UK10:US3) needles
Knitters' pins and a blunt-ended needle
for sewing up
Tweezers (optional)
Acrylic toy stuffing
2 small buttons

FINISHED SIZE

Orangutan measures 6in (15cm) high

TENSION

26 sts x 34 rows measure 4in (10cm)
square over st-st using 3.25mm needles
and DK yarn before stuffing.

ABBREVIATIONS

See page 156

SPECIAL ABBREVIATION

w1: wrap 1 stitch – take yarn between
needles to opposite side, slip 1 stitch
pwise from LH needle to RH needle, then
take yarn between needles to first side.

HOW TO MAKE ORANGUTAN

BODY

Using the long tail method and yarn A, cast on 32 sts.

Row 1: Purl.

Row 2: K7, (m1, k1) 4 times, k11, (m1, k1) 4 times, k6 (40 sts).

Rows 3 to 17: Work 15 rows in st-st.

Rows 18 and 19: Work 2 rows in g-st for waist.

Rows 20 to 29: Beg with a k row, work 10 rows in st-st.

Row 30: K1, (k8, k3tog, k8) twice, k1, (36 sts).

Row 31: Purl.

Row 32: K1, (k7, k3tog, k7) twice, k1, (32 sts).

Row 33: Purl.

Cast off.

HEAD

Using the long tail method and yarn A, cast on 32 sts.

Row 1: Purl.

Row 2: (Kfb, k1) to end (48 sts).

Rows 3 to 15: Work 13 rows in st-st.

Row 16: (K2tog, k4) to end (40 sts).

Row 17 and foll 3 alt rows: Purl.

Row 18: (K2tog, k3) to end (32 sts).

Row 20: (K2tog, k2) to end (24 sts).

Row 22: (K2tog, k1) to end (16 sts).

Row 24: (K2tog) to end (8 sts). Break yarn and thread through sts on needle, pull tight and secure by threading yarn a second time through sts.

MUZZLE

Using the long tail method and yarn B, cast on 20 sts.

Row 1: Purl.

Row 2: K1, (m1, k2) to last st, m1, k1 (30 sts).

Rows 3 to 7: Work 5 rows in st-st.

Row 8: K4, (k2tog) 4 times, k6, (k2tog) 4 times, k4 (22 sts).

Row 9: Purl.

Row 10: K2, (k2tog) 4 times, k2, (k2tog) 4 times, k2 (14 sts).

Row 11: Purl.

Cast off.

FACE PIECE

Using the long tail method and yarn C, cast on 8 sts.

Row 1: Purl.

Row 2: K1, (m1, k1) to end (15 sts).

Rows 3 to 7: Work 5 rows in st-st.

Row 8: (K2tog) twice, k7, (k2tog) twice (11 sts).

Row 9: Purl.

Row 10: (K2tog) twice, k3, (k2tog) twice (7 sts).

Row 11: Purl.

Break yarn and thread through sts on needle, pull tight and secure by threading yarn a second time through sts.

NOSE

Using the long tail method and yarn B, cast on 6 sts.

Rows 1 to 4: Beg with a p row, work 4 rows in st-st, ending with a k row.

Break yarn and thread through sts on needle, pull tight and secure by threading yarn a second time through sts.

DUNGAREES

Using the long tail method and yarn D, cast on 32 sts.

Row 1 and foll 2 alt rows: Purl.

Row 2: K5, (m1, k2) 4 times, k8, (m1, k2) 4 times, k3 (40 sts).

Row 4: K7, (m1, k2) 4 times, k12, (m1, k2) 4 times, k5 (48 sts).

Row 6: K9, (m1, k2) 4 times, k16, (m1, k2) 4 times, k7 (56 sts).

Rows 7 to 19: Work 13 rows in st-st.

Rows 20 to 22: Work 3 rows in g-st, ending with a RS row.

DIVIDE FOR BIB

Row 23: Cast off 21 sts kwise, k13 (14 sts now on RH needle), cast off rem 21 sts kwise and fasten off.

Rejoin yarn to rem sts and patt:

Row 24: K2, (k1 tbl) 10 times, k2 (14 sts).

Row 25: K2, p10, k2.
Row 26: Knit.
Rows 27 to 30: Rep rows 25 and 26 twice more, ending with a k row.
Rows 31 and 32: Work 2 rows in g-st, ending with a RS row.
Cast off in g-st.

LEGS (make 2)

Using the long tail method and yarn D, cast on 10 sts.
Row 1: Purl.
Row 2: (Kfb) to end (20 sts).
Rows 3 to 7: Work 5 rows in st-st.
Row 8: K16, w1 (see special abbreviation), turn.
Row 9: S1p, p12, w1, turn.
Row 10: S1k, k to end.
Row 11: Purl.
Rows 12 to 15: Work 4 rows in g-st.
Rows 16 and 17: Change to yarn A and k 1 row then p 1 row.
Rows 18 to 29: Rep rows 8 to 11, 3 times more.
Row 30: (K2tog, k2) to end (15 sts).
Row 31: Purl.
Row 32: (K2tog, k1) to end (10 sts).
Break yarn and thread through sts on needle, pull tight and secure by threading yarn a second time through sts.

FEET (make 2)

Using the long tail method and yarn C, cast on 8 sts.
Row 1: Purl.
Row 2: (Kfb) to end (16 sts).
Rows 3 to 7: Work 5 rows in st-st.
Row 8: K6, m1, k4, m1, k6 (18 sts).
Row 9: Purl.
Row 10: K6, cast off 6 sts (7 sts now on RH needle), k to end (12 sts).
Rows 11 to 13: Push rem sts together and work 3 rows in st-st.
Row 14: (K2tog) to end (6 sts).
Break yarn and thread through sts on needle, pull tight and secure by threading yarn a second time through sts.

PAWS AND FOREARMS (make 2)

Using the long tail method and yarn A, cast on 10 sts.
Rows 1 to 5: Beg with a p row, work 5 rows in st-st.
Row 6: K1, m1, k to last st, m1, k1 (12 sts).
Rows 7 to 11: Work 5 rows in st-st.
Rows 12 to 23: Rep rows 6 to 11 twice more (16 sts).

Change to yarn C and shape:
Row 24: K6, m1, k4, m1, k6 (18 sts).
Rows 25 to 29: Work 5 rows in st-st.
Row 30: K6, cast off 6 sts (7 sts now on RH needle), k to end (12 sts).
Rows 31 to 33: Push rem sts together and work 3 rows in st-st.
Row 34: (K2tog) to end (6 sts).
Break yarn and thread through sts on needle, pull tight and secure by threading yarn a second time through sts.

STRAPS FOR DUNGAREES (make 2)

Using the long tail method and yarn D, cast on 30 sts.
Row 1: Knit.
Cast off kwise.

MAKING UP

Note: Sew up all row-end seams on right side using mattress stitch one stitch in from the edge, unless otherwise stated; a one-stitch seam allowance has been allowed for this.

BODY

Sew up side edges of body and with this seam at centre back, oversew cast-on stitches. Stuff body leaving neck open.

HEAD

Sew up side edges of head and stuff. Pin and sew head to body making a horizontal stitch over one stitch from head, then a horizontal stitch over one stitch from body and do this alternately all the way round.

MUZZLE AND FACE PIECE

Sew up side edges of muzzle and with this seam at centre of underneath, sew across cast-off stitches and stuff. Arrange muzzle and face piece on face and pin and sew in place.

NOSE

Sew outside edge of nose to top of muzzle leaving a gap, stuff with tweezers or tip of scissors and sew up gap.

DUNGAREES

Sew up side edges of dungarees and with this seam at centre of back, sew across cast-on stitches. Place dungarees on Orangutan. Sew dungarees to row above waist using back-stitch.

LEGS AND FEET

Gather round cast-on stitches of legs, pull tight and secure. Sew up side edges of legs leaving a gap, stuff and sew up gap. Assemble Orangutan on a flat surface and sew legs to sides of body. Fold cast-off stitches of big toe in half and sew up and fasten off. Sew up side edges of feet and stuff feet and big toe with tweezers or tip of scissors. Fold cast-on stitches in half and oversew. Pin and sew feet to legs.

PAWS AND FOREARMS

Fold cast-off stitches of thumb in half and sew up and fasten off. Sew up side edges of hand and place a small ball of stuffing into paws and stuff thumb with tweezers or tip of scissors. Sew up side edges of forearms and stuff as you sew, but leave ½in (1.25cm) at top of arms unstuffed. Sew forearms to body of Orangutan at each side.

STRAPS FOR DUNGAREES AND BUTTONS

Sew ends of straps to bib, take straps over shoulders, cross over and sew to back waist. Add two buttons to bib.

FEATURES

Mark position of eyes with two pins and embroider eyes in black making a vertical chain stitch for each eye, then a second chain stitch on top of first. Embroider eyebrows in black using long stitches. Embroider mouth using long stitches (see page 155 for how to begin and fasten off invisibly for the embroidery).

TECHNIQUES

GETTING STARTED

BUYING YARN

The patterns for the designs in this book are worked in double knitting (or light worsted in the US). There are many yarns on the market, from natural fibres to acrylic blends. Acrylic yarn is a good choice as it washes without shrinking, but always follow the care instructions on the ball band. Be cautious about using a brushed or mohair-type yarn if the toy is intended for a baby or a very young child, as the fibres can be swallowed.

SAFETY ADVICE

Some of the toys have small pieces and trimmings, which could present a choking hazard. Make sure that small parts are sewn down securely before giving any of the toys to a baby or young child.

TENSION

All the toys in this book are knitted on 3.25mm (UK10:US3) knitting needles. This should turn out at approximately 26 stitches and 34 rows over 4in (10cm) square. If there are fewer stitches, the stuffing might show through the fabric and look unsightly. If you use smaller needles the knitting will become tighter.

SLIP KNOT

1. Wind the yarn from the ball round your left index finger from front to back and then to front again. Slide the loop from your finger and pull the new loop through from the centre. Place this loop from back to front onto the needle that is in your right hand.

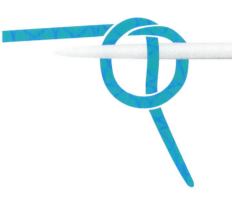

2. Pull the tail of yarn down to tighten the knot slightly and pull the yarn from the ball to form a loose knot.

CASTING ON
(using the long tail method)

1. Leave a long length of yarn: as a rough guide, allow ⅜in (1cm) for each stitch to be cast on plus an extra length for sewing up. Make a slip knot.

2. Hold the needle in your right hand with your index finger on the slip knot loop to keep it in place. Wrap the loose tail end round your left thumb, from front to back. Push the needle's point through the thumb loop from front to back. Wind the ball end of the yarn round the needle from left to right.

3. Pull the loop through the thumb loop, then remove your thumb. Gently pull the new loop tight using the tail yarn.

Repeat this process until the required number of stitches are on the needle.

1

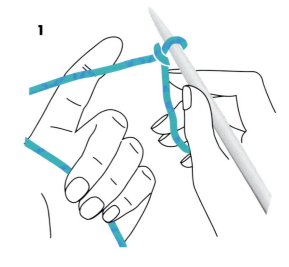

2

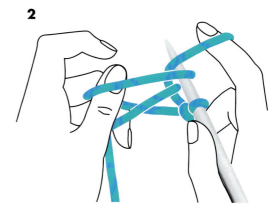

3

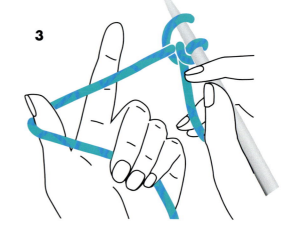

KNITTING STITCHES

KNIT STITCH

1. Hold needle with stitches in left hand. Hold yarn at back of work and insert point of right-hand empty needle into the front loop of the first stitch. Wrap yarn around point of right-hand needle in a clockwise direction using your index finger.

2. With yarn still wrapped around the point, bring the right-hand needle back towards you through the loop of the first stitch. Try to keep the free yarn fairly taut but not too slack or tight.

3. Finally, with the new stitch firmly on the right-hand needle, gently pull the old stitch to the right and off the tip of the left-hand needle. Repeat for all the knit stitches across the row.

PURL STITCH

1. Hold needles with stitches in left hand and hold yarn at front of work.

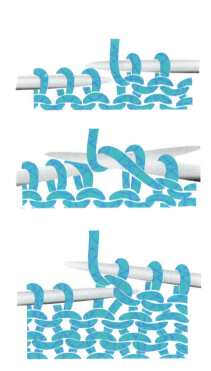

2. Insert point of right-hand empty needle into the front loop of the first stitch. Wrap yarn around point of right-hand needle in an anticlockwise direction using index finger. Bring yarn back to front of work.

3. Now with yarn still wrapped around point of right-hand needle, bring it back through the stitch. Try to keep free yarn taut but not too slack or tight. Finally, with the new stitch firmly on the right-hand needle, gently pull the old stitch off the tip of the left-hand needle. Repeat for all the purl stitches along the row.

GARTER STITCH (A)

This is made by knitting every row.

STOCKING STITCH (B)

Probably the most commonly used stitch in knitting, this is created by knitting on the right side and purling on the wrong side.

REVERSE STOCKING STITCH (C)

This is made in the same way as stocking stitch but the reverse side is the right side.

SHAPING

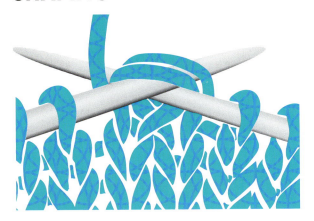

DECREASING

To decrease a stitch, when instructed k2tog or p2tog, simply work two stitches together to make one stitch out of the two stitches. Or if the instructions say k3tog or p3tog, then work three stitches together to make one out of the three.

To achieve a neat appearance to your finished work, this is done as follows:

At the beginning of a knit row and throughout the row, k2tog by knitting two stitches together through the front of the loops (as shown above).

At the end of a knit row, if these are the very last two stitches in the row, then knit together through the back of the loops.

At the beginning of a purl row, if these are the very first stitches in the row, then purl together through the back of the loops. Purl two together along the rest of the row through the front of the loops.

INCREASING

Two methods are used in this book for increasing the number of stitches: m1 and kfb.

M1 Make a stitch by picking up the horizontal loop between the needles and placing it onto the left-hand needle. Now knit into the back of it to twist it on a knit row, or purl into the back of it on a purl row.

Kfb Make a stitch on a knit row by knitting into the front then back of the next stitch. To do this, simply knit into the next stitch but do not slip it off. Take the point of the right-hand needle around and knit again into the back of the stitch before removing the loop from the left-hand needle. You now have made two stitches out of one.

KNITTING ON STITCHES

(or two-needle casting on)

1. Insert the right-hand needle from front to back between the first and second stitches on the left-hand needle and wrap the yarn around the tip of the right-hand needle from back to front.

2. Slide the right-hand needle through to the front to catch the new loop of yarn.

3. Place the new loop of yarn onto the left-hand needle, inserting the left-hand needle from front to back. Repeat this process until you have reached the required number of cast-on stitches.

INTARSIA

Blocks of colour are worked using the intarsia technique. Twist the two different yarns together at the back of the work with each colour change to prevent holes appearing. Once finished, weave in ends at the back of the work.

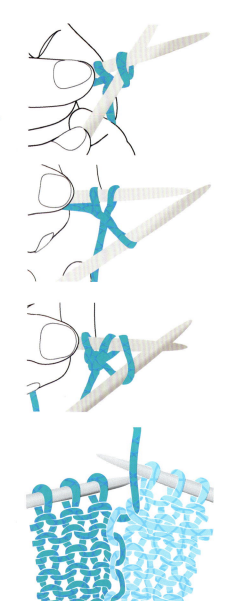

CASTING OFF

1. Knit two stitches onto the right-hand needle, then slip the first stitch over the second and let it drop off the needle. One stitch remains on the needle.

2. Knit another stitch so you have two stitches on the right-hand needle again.

Repeat the process until only one stitch is left on the left-hand needle. Break the yarn, thread it through the remaining stitch and pull tight to fasten off.

SPECIAL INSTRUCTIONS

THREADING YARN THROUGH STITCHES

Sometimes the instructions will tell you to 'thread yarn through stitches on needle, pull tight and secure'. To do this, first break the yarn, leaving a long end, and thread a blunt-ended sewing needle with this end. Pass the needle through all the stitches on the knitting needle, slipping each stitch off the knitting needle in turn. Draw the yarn through the stitches. To secure, pass the needle once again through all the stitches in a complete circle and pull tight.

MAKING-UP INSTRUCTIONS

MATTRESS STITCH (A)

Join row ends by taking small straight stitches back and forth on the right side of work, one stitch from the edge.

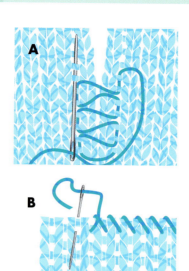

OVER-SEWING (B)

Pieces can also be joined by over-sewing on the wrong side and turning the piece right side out. For smaller pieces or pieces that cannot be turned, oversew on the right side.

BACKSTITCH (C)

Bring needle out at the beginning of the stitch line, make a small stitch and bring the needle out slightly further along the stitch line. Insert the needle at the end of the first stitch and bring it out still further along the stitch line. Continue in the same way to create a line of joined stitches.

STUFFING AND AFTERCARE

Spend a little time stuffing your knitted toy evenly. Acrylic toy stuffing is ideal for this; make sure to use plenty, but not so much that it stretches the knitted fabric so the stuffing can be seen through the stitches. Tweezers are useful for stuffing small parts.

Washable filling is recommended for all the stuffed toys so that you can hand-wash them with a non-biological detergent. Do not spin or tumble dry, but gently squeeze the excess water out, arrange the toy into its original shape, and leave it to dry.

FINISHING TOUCHES

TWISTED CORD

1. Cut even strands of yarn to the number and length stated in the pattern and knot each end. Anchor one end: you could tie it to a door handle or chair, or ask a friend to hold it for you.

2. Take the other end and twist until it is tightly wound.

3. Hold the centre of the cord, and place the two ends together. Release the centre, so the two halves twist together. Smooth it out and knot the ends together.

EMBROIDERY

To begin embroidery invisibly, tie a knot in the end of the yarn. Take a large stitch through the work, coming up to begin the embroidery. Allow the knot to disappear through the knitting and be caught in the stuffing. To fasten off invisibly, sew a few stitches back and forth through the work, inserting the needle where the yarn comes out.

CHAIN STITCH

Bring the needle up through your work to start the first stitch and hold down the thread with the left thumb. Now insert the needle in the same place and bring the point out a short distance away. Keeping the working thread under the needle point, pull the loop of thread to form a chain.

STEM STITCH

Starting at the left-hand side and working towards the right-hand side, work small stitches backwards along the stitch line with the thread always emerging on the same side of the previous stitch.

STRAIGHT STITCH

Come up to start the embroidery at one end of the stitch then go back down at the end of the stitch, coming up in a different place to start the next stitch.

SATIN STITCH

Work a series of straight stitches closely together.

ABBREVIATIONS

alt   alternate

approx   approximately

beg   beginning

cm   centimetre(s)

cont   continue

dec   decrease/decreasing

DK   double knitting

foll   following

g-st   garter stitch: knit every row

g   gram(s)

inc   increase/increasing

k   knit/knitting

k2tog or k3tog   knit two or three stitches together: if these are the very last row, then work through back of loops

kfb   make two stitches out of one: knit into the front then the back of the next stitch

kwise   knitwise

LH   left hand

m1   make one stitch: pick up horizontal loop between the needles and work into the back of it to twist it

mm   millimetre(s)

p   purl

p2tog or p3tog   purl two or three stitches together: if these stitches are the very first in the row, then work together through back of loops

patt   pattern

pwise   purlwise

rem   remaining

rep   repeat(ed)

rev st-st   reverse stocking stitch: purl on the right side, knit on the wrong side

RH   right hand

RS   right side

s1k   slip one stitch knitwise

s1p   slip one stitch purlwise

st(s)   stitch(es)

st-st   stocking stitch: knit on the right side, purl on the wrong side

tbl   through back of loop(s)

tog   together

WS   wrong side

Yf   yarn forward

( )   repeat instructions between brackets as many times as instructed

* or **   repeat from * or ** as instructed

CONVERSIONS

KNITTING NEEDLES

UK	Metric	US
10	3.25mm	3

YARN WEIGHT

UK	US
Double knitting	Light worsted

TERMINOLOGY

UK	US
Cast off	Bind off
Stocking stitch	Stockinette stitch
Tension	Gauge
Anticlockwise	Counterclockwise

INDEX

ACKNOWLEDGEMENTS

Very many thanks to all at GMC who made this book possible. And thanks to friends and family who liked the designs, and special thanks to Cynthia and Helen, from my local wool shop (www.clarewools.co.uk).

DEDICATED TO

Rhiannon Powell

First published 2025 by
Guild of Master Craftsman Publications Ltd,
Castle Place, 166 High Street, Lewes, East Sussex,
BN7 1XU, UK

Text © Sarah Keen, 2025
Copyright in the Work © GMC Publications Ltd, 2025

ISBN 978 1 78494 693 7

All rights reserved

The right of Sarah Keen to be identified as the author of this work has been asserted in accordance with the Copyright, Designs and Patents Act 1988, sections 77 and 78.

No part of this publication may be reproduced, stored in a retrieval system or transmitted in any form or by any means without the prior permission of the publisher and copyright owner.

This book is sold subject to the condition that all designs are copyright and are not for commercial reproduction without the permission of the designer and copyright owner.

While every effort has been made to obtain permission from the copyright holders for all material used in this book, the publishers will be pleased to hear from anyone who has not been appropriately acknowledged and to make the correction in future reprints.

The publishers and author can accept no legal responsibility for any consequences arising from the application of information, advice or instructions given in this publication.

A catalogue record for this book is available from the British Library.

Publisher Jonathan Bailey
Production Jim Bulley
Senior Project Editor Sara Harper
Pattern Checker Jude Roust
Design Manager Robin Shields
Designer Hanri Van Wyk
Photography Andrew Perris

Colour origination by GMC Reprographics
Printed and bound in China

To order a book, contact:
GMC Publications Ltd
Castle Place, 166 High Street,
Lewes, East Sussex, BN7 1XU,
United Kingdom
Tel: +44 (0)1273 488005
www.gmcbooks.com